The Bishop Norris Church of England Secondary School, Tulse Hill

Religious Knowledge *Prize*

Awarded to E. Tharg IVᵇ

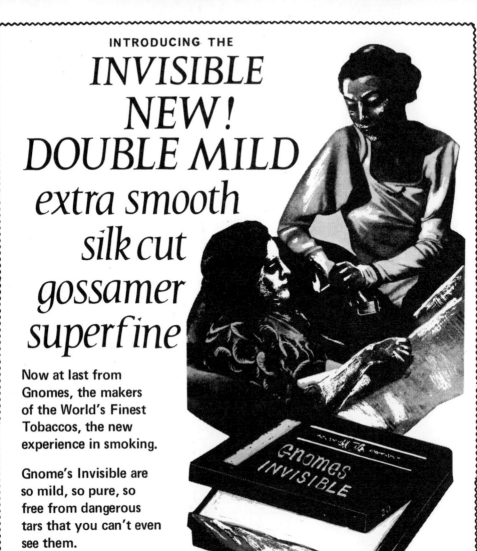

The Best of

PRIVATE EYE

or
A LOAD OF OLD RUBBISH

1974

A PRIVATE EYE BOOK
with
ANDRÉ DEUTSCH·LONDON

Published in Great Britain by Private Eye Productions Ltd,
34 Greek Street, London W1 in association with
André Deutsch Ltd, 105 Great Russell Street, London WC1.

SBN 233 96612 9

Made and Printed in Great Britain by
A. Wheaton & Co, Exeter, Devon

Why is Humphrey Lyttelton wearing the biggest smile in Europe ?

Impressed by Humphrey Lyttelton's fearless and outspoken attacks on eating places in various fashionable magazines, we asked him how much he would want to write a series of drooling, sycophantic puffs for some of the most unpleasant restaurants in the world. "£10,000" came back his reply, quick as the service in a Trust House Forte Kardomah. "O.K." we replied, "you're on." And here's the result.

La Fortorama
Watford Gap

If like me, when you're driving down the M.1., you sometimes feel a bit peckish, you could do a great deal worse than try this gourmet's paradise in steel and glass - with its breathtaking panorama of the non-stop traffic below. I have

Kitchen Manager Norris

been to the Tour D'Argent, the Four Seasons, the Maison Blezard-Levin in the little Dordogne village of St. Muzac, with its coveted 3-stars in Michelin - but I assure you, not one of them can do Golden Texas-Style Farm Fresh Fried Eggs, with Krispy-Brown Sizzling French Fried Potatoes Garnished With Spring-Fresh Water-Washed Sprig of Cress like "Signor" Fred Norris, the kitchen manager at the Fortorama. And all for 95p. Amazing!

The Kardomeramah
Arndale Centre, Cleethorpes

Well, been out East and seen a few things in my time - but I assure nothing like the sweet trolley they bring you in this oasis of good living on the windy shores of the North Sea. Mouth-watering, syrup covered

Manager Trevor Bastard

Banana Gaffes. Handsome chunks of jungle-fresh pineapple, swimming in a bowl of sugary water. Great slabs of Individual Fruit Pie, in all sizes, tastes and colours - and when they say 'individual' they mean it! And finally, the specialité de la maison, rich roly-poly golden-brown-chocolate covered eclairs, made of recycled cardboard - and oozing with great gobs of fresh Cornish Clotted Cream, straight from the local chemical factory. An experience to remember - and you'll have change from a fiver! How they do it beats me.

The Whistler Room

When they had to knock down the famous old Café des Pseuds to build a new skyscraper, what a brilliant idea it was to recreate the old Café - with all its memories and associations - on the 28th floor. Here you can still see Oscar Wilde's toothpick, unused since 1895. Here also are framed reproductions of 'Spy' cartoons, showing many of the famous literary figures of the period. And here too, if you are lucky, you may catch a glimpse of some of the wits and

Receptionist Beryl Maudling

literary lions of our own time - myself, William Davis or Clement Freud - lunching on our expense accounts. Believe me, the atmosphere hasn't changed a jot since a penniless Augustus John was in here selling his sketches for half-a-crown a time to pay his bar bill! Try the *Oeufs Mazarin de Richelieu de Chateaubriand Frites D'or A La Texas Style Avec Des Pommes Frites A La Watford Gap Garni Avec Un Morceau de Cresson*, for a mere £3.55 And if you are a lover of fine claret, as I confess I am, I highly recommend the Chateau Victor Rothschild 1927 at a ridiculous £34.60 a half-bottle (excluding VAT). All this, and an eye level view of Centre Point too? Amazing!

Head Waiter Mario Martini

The Royal-Air-Forte (Heathrow).

What a brilliant idea to convert this old underground aircraft hanger into an exact replica of Chatsworth - so that American tourists can step straight off their jumbo jets, and need never step outside London Airport! Here are genuine smoke-blackened old beams shipped straight from Tokyo (mind your head!) You can sip a cocktail in an exact replica of the cabin where Nelson died on H.M.S. Victorious. And, wow, you should just see the food. Real down-to-earth traditional British farm-kitchen Texas-style cooking of the kind you only dream about. Just taste those scrumptious, sizzling golden-fresh eggs, straight from the Watford Gap! And get an eyeful of that sweet-trolley. The oozy-rich, luscious 'n lovely, syrup-soaked Banana Gaffes. Those jungle-juicy, coral-kissed pineapple chunks swimming in (contd.M. 94)

Doorman 'Arnie'

I AM FIRST MAN TO SET FOOT IN CENTREPOINT

by Lunchtime O'Booze

Somewhere in Central London, Friday.

Towering above us into the darkness loomed the great mass of masonry which has baffled mankind for centuries.

Each one of the 200 men standing here in its shadow knew that at long last one of the greatest enigmas in man's history was about to yield up its inmost secret to the waiting world.

INDESCRIBABLE TENSION

For centuries legends had accumulated, like the sands of the desert, round this strange, vast and mysterious obelisk, set in the middle of London.

Who built it? What was it for? What did the great mass of stone contain?

YES

One widely held view is that Centre Point was never intended for human occupation, but was simply a "cult object", built as a symbol of the worship of office blocks which flourished during the reign of Eheath l, the so-called "Grocer King".

Local legend has long associated the building with the mysterious figure of Harry Hyams, a semi-mythical creature, half-faun, half-man, whom it was said no human being had ever set eyes on.

But perhaps the most sinister of all the local superstitions about Centre Point was that which told of the presence of the so-called Abominable Goodman.

From time to time, apparently, travellers had caught glimpses near the building of a huge, hairy, ape-like creature with the shambling gait of a gorilla, quite unlike anything known to science.

TSCHAIKOWSKY

At last, at 5.30 yesterday afternoon, Centre Point was about to yield up the answer to these and a thousand other baffling riddles.

After years of careful planning, the great Gnome Centrepoint Expedition arrived at last at the huge slab of glass which for hundreds of years had barred the way to the heart of the great Hyams enigma.

With us was a huge, chattering, mob of local tribesmen—bearded Maoites, excited

Trotskyites with their flowing robes and long hair, Camden Councillors and chanting, bald-pated worshippers of Hare Krishna, who for years past have held their strange rites at the foot of the building.

TREVOR ROPER

In an atmosphere of intense excitement, we broke through the final barrier—and at last stood in the Forbidden Citadel!

As our eyes became accustomed to the gloom, we could see huge, rusting metal columns, acres of dusty chambers stretching up and up into the sky, and everywhere the dank, musty smell of decay.

Scraping away centuries of grime, I could just make out an inscription in ancient hiero-glyphics which read:

"This VERY WONDERFUL OFFICE BLOCK was designed by R. Seifert & Partners, Holborn 2346 (8 lines)—Telegrams & Cables GROTBLOX. Anything legal considered."

But of the legendary Hyams himself and the Abominable Goodman there was no sign.

Just the eerie darkness and the moaning of the wind.

YOUR VAT CORNER

OLD BORE WRITES

If you 'aven't had a chance already now's the toime when you get round to it to get out all those old VAT returns and take a good look at 'em. First of all make sure your output zero rating doesn't equal your input surface tax. This is most important because if you go wrong here it'll mean trouble galore in months ahead.

And keep an eye on the way non-taxable discounts, especially those at 4% or under in the £1 relate to deductable surcharge increments. These can be tricky little customers when it comes down to it and if you let it go boy now there's no tellin' what moight 'appen. There's an old saying worth remembering, "Pro-rata invoice charging, remember, comes at the beginning of November." One last tip from an old VAT hand: Don't fill those VAT forms in too quick loike. If you do, it'll go wrong and they'll only send it back to you and you'll have to start all over again.

Cheeriohohohoho! Best o' luck!

Cecil Beaton

Continuing our serialisation of the witty, urbane and enthralling memories of one of the most fascinating figures of our time.

The Years of Insufferable Hardship

1948~1953

Ah! To be in Neasd-en-Provence during the saison. I motored to the Chateau Pomfritte where I am the guest of Buffy and Duffy Godber. Buffy is radiant, as always in a mauve chiffon mou-mou and huge picture hat. She adores la France.

"Look at the trees" she says. "And the sky. It's all so natural. Things growing."

Later I wait in Duffy's bedroom while he is dressing for the Moet-Chandon's fancy-dress motor-rally. He has just come back from Venice where he has been filming with Diana Mayne-Baring and Gerald du Balon in Larry's "Fantasie de Peking".

As we are talking Buffy interrupts our tete-a-tete bringing in a glass of vino tinto.

"I say. Has anyone seen my woolly drawers?"

We all laugh. Buffy's maid, a hideous little Mulatto from God knows where bring: in a note from Archie saying that Greta Chevrolet is waiting in the hall and would love to see me.

Greta! What a joy to behold her again. Quelle beaute! She gives a ravishing smile.

"Well well. You are a naughty boy.

LADY MARLENE WORSTHORNE
"Never the same after Beverley's marriage"

BUFFY & DUFFY GODBER
"Delightfully rude to the servants"

Where are your trousers?"

Buffy (British Consul in Limoges) throws back his head and laughs hysterically.

"No one wears trousers south of the Poisson" he cries.

"Oh don't they?" Rita replies. What a wit Rita can be when she wants to. Buffy sulks in a corner. He doesn't know what to put on.

"Come on Cecil" he says at last. "You know all about fashion. How do I do up my shoe-laces?"

The phone rings. It is Vaseline calling from San Francisco asking me to design a new production of Victor Bemax's ballet "Les Matelots Mechants" with La Ballsova and Leonid Muesli.

Breakfast with Nigel Goring and his beautiful wife Enid. They want to know all the news from Newport Pagnell.

Motored to Hampshire for lunch with Candida, who to everyone's surprise has just announced her engagement to Winston Churchill.

She is so happy, and as amusing as ever "Hullo, sailor!" she greets me. Everybody laughs, I can't think why. Perhaps it's just her tone of voice when she says it.

After lunch she drove me to Dempster's, the charming residence which Lutyens did up for Lord Waitrose after his aunt Lady Emerald Jarvis went down in the Aspidistra.

She and Winston are planning to move in after their wedding. Candy wants me to suggest colours for the curtains. "Winnie hates anything dark. He loves bright plain colours-you know, red, yellow, blue, green, that sort of thing".

In the conservatory we found Duffy and Buffy deep in conversation with Kevin Waugh and Angie Disprin, the half-brother of Dulcie Levin.

"Hullo everyone" announces Candida. "I've brought Cecil over for a game of tennis."

"But I haven't brought my racket" I said.

They all laugh and throw cakes at me.

TENNIS AT DROPPINGS
(L to R) Reggie Twytte, Lord Longford, Steve Pomfret, Rayner Heppenstall

Next week: I photograph the Duke Of Gloucester: Why are his clothes so dreary? As told to William Davis

SID AND DORIS 'LIKE A PACK OF ANIMALS'

— Neasden Chairman

by E.I. Addio Our Man in the Casualty Ward
With the Enlarged Liver and the Fractured Elbow

"In twenty five years of soccer I have seen nothing like it" lashed out an ashen-faced Ron Knee, 59, from his Neasden Bridge HQ last night.

Supremo Knee's shock outburst followed Saturday's unprecedented scenes involving the Neasden fans Sid and Doris Bonkers.

LOYALTY

Trouble started when Neasden Number 4 Shirt, Len Essoldo, was sent off by Referee Sid Himmler in a controversial decision.

As the Neasden player walked off plainly incensed at Referee Himmler's harsh verdict, the fans Sid and Doris swarmed onto 'the park' tearing up the turf with their bare hands and throwing it at players and referee alike.

BLITZ

Police (PC "Ned" Strangelove, or the Odd Copper as he is known) were powerless to prevent the marauding horde from turning the Neasden Bridge Road Stadium into something resembling the aftermath of Hiroshima.

Goalposts were torn out and set fire to, while custodian Foot, W., slept on oblivious of the holocaust that was raging.

Armed with home made anti-tank missiles the two-strong maelstrom surged towards the directors' box where a terrified Neasden chairman, local launderama magnate Brig. "Buffy" Cohen pleaded with them over the public address system, offering the enraged supporters free laundry facilities for a week if they would return quietly to the terraces.

ARMAGEDDON

But the trail of terror did not stop at the stadium.

Boarding the 9.30 Neasden-Gunnersbury Park Soccer Special, the angry swarm of supporters ripped up fixtures and fittings in a mad frenzy of football fanatacism which a British Rail spokesman described as "the actions of human savages running amok like a pack of hungry okapis".

POST MORTEM

Yesterday Neasden club officials racked their brains in an effort to find a solution to what they are calling "the Blight of the Bonkers."

One suggestion from the Chairman Brig. Cohen is to provide special luxury padded cell-style stands in which the fans could relax in conditions of 4-star anaesthesia.

But "Big Ron" Knee, the 59 year old master-mind takes a different view.

"Like talks to like" says the tight lipped Super-Brain. "They should be forced to train for half an hour at the Bridge with the squad. A 'touch-on' from Baldy for example would help them re-think their whole attitude to hooliganism in the seventies."

Ron Knee is 59.

Late Score

Raynes Pk Rovers...9 Neasden....0
(Pevsner (o.g.) 5,
Lycett-Green 2
Aspler 2)

Pitch condition: Scorched

"Truly remarkable - just as predicted on the box."

Gnoming, Gnoming,

Private Eye today launches a major series intended to provide an authoritative guide to the increasingly complex and baffling world of the World of Antiques.

Every year, as more and more antiques fall on the floor and get broken, the stock of genuine-style *objets d'art* diminishes,

1940-1941

THE ACME LION

Acme Mangle by Ongar Muesli. Muesli takes the simple structure of a wash mangle and turns it into something extremely boring. Dismissed in his time as a mere Acme Mangle Designer, Muesli is now much prized by Mangle Collectors throughout the world. "This one will wring and wring." F.C. **£860**

Wireless Set c 1940 designed by Gustav Münch at his Stevenage workshop and manufactured by Electrical Wireless Ltd. Münch defied the conventions of his day by failing to provide an ON/OFF switch, hence the fact that these sets are now rare. Brown plastic case, hessian-style speaker-cover. **£350**

Suit case 1921 by Leonhardt Bruchmeister. Now in the British Rail Museum of Lost Property, this miniature trunk was considered very ordinary in its time. Cover hinges show influence of the pre-Raphaelites. **£150**

'Concertina' Camera by Fergus van der Migran. Little can be said about this object which won the coveted Prix de Trasch in 1940. **£1,940**

Electric Bedside Lamp and Clock in Chrome and Machine-Stitched Plastex by Imogen Süssmeyer. Here we see Süss-meyer's imaginative use of plastex and chrome. **£250-£300**

Upholstered armchair by Bevis Hillier. Hillier was a founder member of the Tottenham Court Road School and this chair with its imaginative use of coil springs and heavy oak frame is considered by many critics to be an ideal way of starting a bonfire. Oak leaf motif by Daphne du Youmindlov harks back to Beloff, Plinth, Hoggmeyer, Bondalini, Mopz, Nagasaki and Meinzadoppeldiamond-Vatvevantisvatnis. **£890**

Gnome! THE PRIVATE EYE GUIDE TO ANTIQUES

and the frontiers of the 'antique' are pushed closer to our own time.

That is why world-famous Lord Gnome has assembled a unique team of experts to compile what we sincerely hope will be a definitive appraisal of this often mystifying subject.

<u>Parker Quink Ink Bottle</u>. Early forties. Glass designed by Heinrich Von Dongen. Fluted Plastic cap by Fritz Neasdling. Echoes Odeon Cinema Architecture of the Period. Now virtually unobtainable. The label is considered to be a masterpiece of 40's graphics and is the work of the young English Ink Bottle Label Graphics Designer Edgar Minns. £750-£800

<u>Shoe by F.Gaudier Brezska</u>. This exquisite leather shoe with crepe soles and laces speaks for itself. Between £40 and £50

<u>Black-cased Car Battery</u> by Oscar Beuselinck. Beuselinck only designed one battery before his tragic death in a battery explosion in 1940. This is a classic period piece showing all the hallmarks of Beuselinck's genius. £450

<u>Chrome Light Fitting</u> with Pink Inflammable Plastic Shades by Edward Lucie-Schmidt. 1940. Schmidt was the star pupil of Daftbügger (1878-1945). This example of Schmidt's early period was commissioned by Luton Wall Fittings Co. Millions were produced and are still to be found in the warehouse of the Luton Wall Fittings Co., Luton, Beds. **10p.**
Hurry! Hurry! While stocks last.

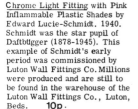

<u>Electric Toaster</u> in Heat-Resistant Aluminium, by the widely-acclaimed Toaster Designer Hovis Wonderlöf. Wonderlöf was the only member of Les Six (The Six). **£103**

Photographs by Laurence Stuttering, Josquin de Malmsey, Nicki Prissfinger. Sources: Victoria and Albert Museum, Ronald Museum (no relation), Lord Clark of Civilisation, St.Botolph's Bring and Buy Sale, Sotheby's, Ron Hall Ltd., (We buy All Old Articles - Best Prices Paid! - TER 1234)

<u>Sunday Times Colour Supplement</u> 1972 by Godfrey Smith and others. Smith and his school pioneered the 'Pull Out Supplement' which could be cut out and kept in expensive binders. The supplements were well known for their trivial glossy appearance and trashy second-hand pseudery about Great Men of the Century, Cinema, Antiques, etc. **2p (o.n.o.)**

"That's what the ploughman has for lunch, fish fingers and chips"

"I think they could have done without a second hand, don't you?"

HONEYSETT.

LONGFORD meets the KRAYS

THANKS TO A MINUTE PRESIDENT NIXON-STYLE BUGGER INSTALLED BY PRIVATE EYE AGENTS, EVERY CONVERSATION IN PARKHURST IS NOW TAPE-RECORDED FOR HISTORICAL ARCHIVES.

THE FOLLOWING IS A TRANSCRIPT OF JUST ONE SUCH HISTORICAL DIALOGUE

Reggie Kray: My bruvver and I would like to begin by saying how truly grateful we both are of your lordship coming to see us like this.

Ronnie Kray: Hullo sailor!

Reggie *(aside):* Belt up Ron or you'll be having your teef for lunch.

As I was saying baldie, that is to say Your Highness me and Ron have seen the light ain't we Ron? Ron? *(Nudging him in ribs)*

Ronnie: Oh yeah. Jesus wants me for a sunbeam. Is that how it goes?

Longford: This is really most encouraging. But you must realise that you both sinned and done wrong.

Reggie: Yeah we realise that we are sinned most grievously.

Ronald: Yeah. Grievously bodily harm in fact.

Reggie: Leave the talking to me you stupid 'Arris or 'e'll tumble it.

Longford: I've brought some books for you to read. There's one I've written myself called 'Humility' which I think is a very good book, and the Holy Bible and Cardinal Heenan's Life Story.

Reggie: We are deeply grateful for your spiritual guidance. It has taken us heavy porridge before we seen the light.

Longford: Our Lord is infinite in his mercy. It doesn't matter how disgusting and horrible you are or to what revolting depths of degradation you have sunk I will come and cheer up on behalf of Our Lord.

Ronnie: Have you got a fag?

Reggie: I've told you once banana brain. We're not conning im for fags or nuffink else. This is the geezer who's come to talk to us about God. Remember now? The man who's going to help us see the light?

Ronnie: Oh, yeah! The toff wot's going to spring us.

(Reggie thumps Ronnie in the mouth)

Longford: Oh dear! This is terribly distressing!

Reggie *(going on knees):* Oh Lord forgive me for I know not what I do.

Longford: Oh dear, look at the time. I must be going. I'm on *Any Questions.* Can I get you anything?

Reggie: Well, since you ask, My Lord, We would like to say that Ronnie and me would dearly love to make a little shrine to Our Lady for our little cell.

Longford: How very touching!

Reggie: Yeah we're glad you fink that. So what we're short of for the job is one of them oxyacetylene welding and cutting jobs which you can pick up anywhere and some workers overalls and possibly if you can run to it a couple of false beards.

Longford *(writing in notebook):* I'll certainly see what I can do. I shall remember you in my prayers.

Reggie: And we're not likely to forget you neither. Are we Ron? You must excuse im your Grace he's a heavy sleeper.

(Exit Longford)

ANGLO SAXON CHRONICLE

Two Groats   28 May 1016

I'm only here for the Beowulf

WEATHER

Sunny

CANUTE It's 'business as usual'

"Trust Me"~ King's Seashore Plea

by WASSAILTIME O'MEAD Weymouth, Tuesday

"I'm not a loser" claimed a wet but triumphant King Canute on the beach here today, as the waves continued to rise around his ornate gold throne.

"I didn't become King of England by ducking tough issues" an ashen-faced Canute told reporters, "and I'm going to sit this one out, come hell or high water."

Knotcase

Already in recent weeks, many of the King's closest advisers-including the men Erlich and Halde - have been swept away by the oncoming waters.

The King is now virtually alone here on the seashore at Weymouth.

Many people feel it is only a matter of time before he himself is engulfed.

But there is no mistaking King Canute's determination to give the impression to outside observers that it is 'business as usual' for the most powerful man in Wessex.

Only yesterday, as the waters reached his chest, he received a delegation of Veterans from the Battle of Ethandune.

In his speech of welcome the king pointedly made no mention of his unusual marine circumstances - although by this time the waves were lapping at his shoulders, and small crustacea were visible adhering to his lower extremities.

Torque-In

"Next month's State Visit by the King of Scotland, MacBrezhneth, is still on", a seaside spokesman said today.

"The Scottish King will go swim-about with King Canute accompanied by thousands of security frogmen, as planned" he stated.

All in all, the word from Weymouth in these confused and turbulent times is that King Canute carries on.

Turning a blind eye to the seaweed and oil slick which is now forming in a thick scum around his beard, the King told me "I am looking forward with confidence to still being here when the Monarchy celebrates its 1000th anniversary in 991 years time."

"In fact", the king went on, "aargl-gaargle - glug-glug."

King Canute was 58.

On other pages

CRICKET

Sir Alec Vass –70 not out!

by E W 'Big Jim' Swansong

Sir Alec Vass is 70 today and there cannot be a single lover of the game who does not wish this great old player Many Happy Returns.

It is heartening, what's more, to know that Alec has no intention of hanging up his bat for the present. He has let it be known that he is available for selection as long as ever he is wanted.

Bravo

There can be few cases of a man who has played so often as 'Baillie'. as we know him in the Long Room, without once scoring a run.

Yet the fact that he has never got off the mark in any of his 8.000 odd innings has in no way lessened his reputation. His prestige I would say is now higher than it has ever been.

Sir Alec first played for England under Chamberlain N. in the disastrous season of 1937. He was out first ball. but his bearing and style endeared him to the hearts of the crowd.

Superb

Alas during the captaincy of W. Churchill (1940-45) Vass was out of action due to an injury.

It was not until the England side was under the leadership of 'Mac' Macmillan that Alec came back into the team, and with characteristic panache scored a succession of ducks which are still spoken of with awe by all those who were lucky enough as I was to have seen them.

It came as no surprise on the retirement of 'Mac' when 'Vassie' took over as captain of England.

Legendary

In many ways it was his finest hour. His

CLEAN BOWLED! Sir Alec yesterday

scores during the period of his captaincy tell their own remarkable story
C. 0. 0. 0. 0. 0. 0 & C.

Brilliant

In more recent times Alec has been quite content to stay on under the new captain and carry on in the same tradition.

As the years passed his reputation on and off the field has grown, until now there is no one in the game who commands a wider degree of respect and admiration.

Today as we salute him on this auspicious occasion he is a living inspiration to every young schoolboy who dreams of one day turning out for his country.

God speed, good luck and well batted!

LOOK!

I JUST DIG THOSE DISHY DONS *drools Jolly Sooper*

Oxford in February. Those spires are certainly dreamy all right. Golden leaves drift down the High Street like shoals of angelfish. Golden crunchy crumpets sizzle by the fire, drooling in butter. So now I'm a broad in the Broad. Geddit?

One of the dishiest dons around these days is gorgeous Tristram de Strange. Suave, dark-eyed, wearing only a russet satin bathrobe and hand-tooled ski boots from Blades, Tristram is an old Etonian who, after a brilliant career in stage design and a tragically brief affair with a Greek waiter in Camden Town, is now the most popular economic history lecturer in Oxford.

His wit is a byword among his fellow dons. In America once, he is reputed to have quipped to a seminar: "We have nothing to lose but our Keynes". Today he sparkles over the High Table port and cheese at Queens College, spraying epigrams like a machine gun over anyone within earshot. As we sat beneath the 14th century portraits, sipping a priceless Nuits St Georges-Weidenfeld-des-Cinq-Femmes, he turned to his next-door neighbour, a nondescript sociologist from New Zealand, and said: "I suppose the luminescence of this delectable burgundy is lost on a grotty little colonial like you". How we all giggled!

Jolly Sooper's Oxford

Outside again into the thin winter sunshine dappling the Bodleian with pinks and greys, where I run into one of the most brilliant of the older generation of dons, Hugh Very-Ropey. He is a suave, grey-haired, gorgeous-ly-distinguished looking figure, in a marvellous, eye-catching anorak from Millett's.

Years ago simply everyone loved his gorgeous pieces in the *Spectator*. I sidled up to him in my best slinky manner, and asked him in a breathy whisper: "Like a nice time dearie?" He seemed quite put out, the old bore. It seems that gorgeous pieces aren't his line any more. Geddit?

Goodbye Isaiah Berlin

Anyway, I soon found consolation, because the next man I went to call on was quite the most exciting thing to hit Oxford since Morrie 'Hotlips' Bowra and Izzy 'Fats' Berlin first blew in from the steppes in 1903. He is the man just everyone's talking about, the sexiest philosopher since Spinoza, Anthony Quinton-Crewe, Senior Tutor at Badger Hall.

Quinton-Crewe is undoubtedly the dishiest thing since Descartes in the philosophy line. A suave, forty-ish teddy bear, who purrs round Oxford in a shell-pink Hispano-Suiza, he lives in a space-age fibreglass caravan on Portmeadow, with his unbelievably slinky and super Phillipino wife, Justine. She is a tremendously talented artist, who

At this point his Saluki, which he has wittily named Danny La Rue because he is not sure of its sex, jumped up on the sofa and started to do unmentionable things with my handbag. We were saved by Justine telling us that lunch was on the table.

Justine Time

Over a breathtakingly mouth-watering plate of tagliatelli, he told me just what modern philosophy was all about. "It's all quite simple" he quipped, through a mouthful of pasta, "Take for instance this delicious glass of Vino Tinto. Now you see it. Now", he went on, knocking it back, "you don't. It's all in the mind, you see!" Even to a saucy little silly-billy like me, it suddenly seemed as if philosophy was the simplest thing in the world.

After lunch we went into his library, which contains an astonishing collection of books, ranging from a complete telephone directory (the famous 1969 edition) to Georgette Heyer. Here he showed me the proofs of his new book, his first, modestly titled *"What It's All About"*

After the Vino Tinto, it was certainly all Greek to me. But as I stumbled out into the breathtaking February sunlight, flecking the mellow stone of the quad with Japanesey pastel tints of puce and saffron, I felt quite limp. After all, it is not every day that you can have lunch with the most brilliant mind of the twentieth century.

© R.'Badger'Hall and J.Sooper 1973.

makes the most marvellous mobiles out of old bus tickets and fir cones.

Over a sexy toothmug-full of Cyprus Neasdillado, Quinton-Crewe told me something about his glamorous life. "Oh, it's nothing really." he said with mouth-watering modesty. "I've just knocked off a few articles here and there, mostly in the *Sunday Telegraph*.

"They pay better than the Proceedings of the Aristotelian Society" he joked, showing a set of perfectly-formed teeth.

" 'In the beginning...'
Are you listening, Hilda?"

VERDICT:
The most disgusting thing I've ever seen

says E.I.ADDIO
Our Man with his hand on the Chairman's wife's knee (no relation)

Fans (Sid and Doris Bonkers) queued all night yesterday for tickets to see what some people are calling the most disgusting show on Earth - Neasden United v Ongar Academicals at the Neasden Bridge Road Stadium.

Let me say this. I have seen some pretty ugly scenes in my 25 years on the terraces.

But for sheer filth this matter beats them all into a cocked hat.

WOUNDED KNEE

Afterwards I spoke to Sid Bonkers. How did he react to the game they are calling the Culloden of Soccer history?

"Frankly I enjoyed it" said Sid. "It was well worth coming all the way from Tesco Road to see."

RELEGATION WORRIES

What did he think of the scenes in which Neasden custodian of the uprights, one-legged Wally Foot, gouged out the eye of Ongar's Number 4 Shirt Bronnie McWaugh.

"I could find nothing disgusting in this act," said Sid, a former youth-club leader. "You can see much worse than this in a lot of games."

PITCH

But what of his wife, Doris? How did a woman react to the incident when referee Sid Himmler's ear was bitten off in a goal-mouth melee?

"I found it very boring" said homely, bespectacled Mrs. Bonkers. "I can't see what all the fuss is about. If people don't want to see soccer like this they should stay away."

Mrs. Bonkers is 47.

LATE SCORE

ONGAR AC.....10 NEASDEN.....0
(McWaugh 3 Osmond 2
Pevsner (og) 4 Cash 1)

Attendance 2   Receipts 50p.

KEVIN
WOODCOCK

Some things in life are too important to care about. A field of corn in June. The
song of a nightingale. The smell of fresh roses after rain.

That's why there are some things one has to think about. Carefully.
In case anything goes wrong.

Advice is not the easiest thing in the world to give someone.
Real advice is a tender thing.

Like a mother smiling at her child. Or water lapping on the sea shore.

So think about it again. After all, it doesn't cost you anything. To sit and wonder....

And don't be frightened of the answers you'll get. It may be difficult at first.
Like a kitten trying to walk.

You don't have to believe us. Just think about it.
Some things in life really are important.

GNOMEX ANTI-VENEREAL
CONTRAPTIONS & DEVICES LTD.

Dept.X, Neasdenwood, Staffs. I am under 21.

Today we begin the serialisation of one of the most remarkable documents in the history of the world. It is the story of the marriage between two of the most astonishing human beings who ever existed—Victoria Station and George Weidenfeld. In the words of their son Nigel Molesworth "It is one of the great love stories of the world".

The Happiest Marriage in the World

INTRODUCTION by the Hon. Nigel Molesworth.

What follows may shock you. But after talking to many of my friends, and in particular my bank manager [**Reginald Braithwaite**], I have decided that it would be wrong for the world to remain ignorant for a second longer of one of the most beautiful marriages in the history of romantic love.

Daddy and Mummy were certainly an odd pair. He was a Roaring Pooftah [**Harold Roaring-Pooftah, one of the Dorset Roaring-Pooftahs**] and she was a Raging Dyke [**Letitia Raging-Dyke, 2nd daughter of the Marquess of Rickmansworth, see picture**]. No two people had ever had less in common. They hated each other with a venomous hatred from the moment they first met. They were seldom together during the seventy four years of their blissfully unhappy marriage. Yet a strange bond held them together. [**Sir Arthur Bond, the celebrated hermaphrodite masseur, who visited them both regularly at their home until the day they finally killed each other**].

The Beginning

I first met Dame Harold Evans when I was out walking with my husband [**Lytton Strachey**]. We were in Hyde Park, I remember. It was a perfect spring day. The pussy-willow buds were out everywhere, and as soon as I met her I knew that I had never come across anyone so remarkable in my life.

She was a small, vibrant man, in a dark suit, talking rather boastfully about her latest ski-ing exploits.

I know now that I have never been so passionately in love with anyone as I was with Dame Harold during those hectic summer months we spent together in Florence [**Dame Florence Horsbrugh, who later became Minister of Works 1953-1955**].

Soon after that [1908] I got married to George [**Weidenfeld, who was in publishing at the time**]. We were staying together in the same house party at Droppings. The King [**Edward VII**] was sleeping with George's mother at the time, and whenever one happened to see someone tip-toeing into her room at 3.00 in the morning, one never knew whether it was the king or the doctor [**Dr. Ephraim Hackenbusch. M.D., with whom she was also having a raging affair at the time**].

In 1909 they all went to stay in Bognor . . .

Dear Diary,

I am in love again. This time Harold is in Italy [**Hector Berlioz 1803—1869**]. Dare I speak my love? She is tall and fair and her name is Frances Wyndham. We met at a house party down at Mellors. It was somehow an enchanted evening. I saw a stranger across a crowded room. And somehow I knew that somewhere I would see her again and again. Once I had found her I would never let her go. Dear diary, can you believe it?

Diary: "Get on with it, you old slag!"

In 1914 the Great War broke out . . .

Frances has written me a letter. It is the most beautiful letter I have received in my life. In fact it is quite different from any other letter I have ever read:

Dear Sir or Madam,

Your name has been selected by our computer from thousands living in your area [**The Grove, Watford Gap** *] . . .*

I was so moved that I couldn't read another word.

© 1973. The executors of the late Bourn-Vita Have-Sack-Vill-Drivel.

People in the picture - front row left to right: Hon. Mrs. Violet Sackville, Sir Eve-rard Vest, Lord Sackville-West, Sir Michael Swann-Vesta-Tilley, Reggie Sackville-West-End-Central, Candida Sackville-Street-Porter, Lady Violet Bonham Carter, Mrs. Vita Wheat West Sackville Street, Hon. Lovely Violets (centre standing): Dame Rebecca West, Lord Gorblimey Savile-Row, Hon. Sacherevell Savile-Sitwell-Sackville, Sit Vac p. 94, Lord Centre Standing West, Victoria de los Station, Queen Victoria Street; (seated) Lord Arthur Savile's crime figures up again (cont. p. 94).

We invite you to accept any three of these exquisitely

FREE as your

ADOLF

Book

They called him 'the most evil man who ever lived'. He left half Europe a smoking heap of rubble. Millions died at his command. And yet, although he has been dead nearly 30 years, this tortured genius will continue to fascinate, hypnotise and puzzle the world to the end of time.

Now you too have a unique opportunity to get to know Adolf Hitler - in the intimacy of your own home. No carpet will be safe from the champing teeth of this monster who spread a trail of havoc across half the civilised world!

Open any one of these books - and just watch as a whole crowd of larger-than-life characters spill out of the pages, to join you at your fireside...

✳ Meet bluff, outsize Hermann Goering, the drug-crazed art collector in a silk dressing gown, who could never say no to an orgy...

✳ Ashen-faced, tight-lipped Josef Goebbels, the club-footed intellectual who dreamed of world domination...

✳ Curvaceous, shy Eva Braun, the 'girl from next door' who washed Hitler's socks during air raids.

These are only a handful of the host of colourful, whacky, fantastic characters who surge through the pages of one of the greatest epics history has ever written. Remember - these people are genuine historical characters. It didn't need a Dostoievsky or a Dickens to dream them up.

Relive again, as it happened only 30 years ago...

✳ The day Hitler set fire to the Reichstag in a fury of megalomania.

✳ Dance with him in the forest of Compiegne, after smashing the armed might of France in only ten minutes...

✳ Hear him whistle Wagner's immortal *Traumerei* in the smoking ruins of the Warsaw Ghetto...

✳ Thrill as he launches a million Panzer divisions into the soft underbelly of the Ukraine...

✳ Weep with him in the Bunker as he searches for his lost ball...

...ound volumes absolutely

...ntroduction to the

HITLER Club

1 THE WATERCOLOURS OF ADOLF HITLER by world-famous art historian Lord Clark. Do these agreeable little landscapes contain the clue to the enigma that was Hitler? Perhaps we shall never know. But these charming vignettes of Viennese life at the turn of the century make one of the most delightful coffee-table books for a long time. *"These ones will run and run"* Windsor and Newton.

2 THE CASE HISTORY OF A. SCHICK-LEGRUBER: *A Diagnostician Gives His Verdict.* by Dr. Johannathan Müller, Researcher in Neurological Disorders, Chichester.
Was Hitler mad? Or just very very sane? A disciple of R.D. Laing comes up with an astonishing answer to the age-old question.

3 THE CARPET BITERS by Harold Robbintrop. Best-selling novelist Robbintrop has written another larger-than-life winner - as in 1837 pages he recreates in every detail the life at Hitler's bizarre mountain-top court. This intimate, highly adult reconstruction of the private lives of the top Nazis is based on years of histori-cal research. *"A rich tapestry of passion and primitive violence woven against the magnificent backdrop of the Bavarian Alps".* Lady Magnesia Freelove.

4 THE HOME-MOVIES OF ADOLF HIT-LER edited by Andrew Sinclair and Francis Wyndham. The first full-length cinematographical study of Hitler's private-ly made films, recently shown for the first time. Could Hitler have been a great Hollywood director? Authors Sinclair and Wyndham leave us in the dark - watching some of the most boring home movies ever recorded on celluloid.

Each volume is hand-printed on special soft-to-the-touch India-style "Papyrotex", and bound in crushed sage leaves hand-picked by slave labourers working for Slater-Walker (SA). Please rush me 240 sets FREE. I promise to pay £2,418.00 next week. I am a megalomaniac bent on world domination.

NAME..............................

ADDRESS..........................

Eating

● Druggy Dave's Indian Drive-In, 479 Finchley Road. Real Indian food and the decor is great. Shredded Kallicharian (49p), a sort of uncooked rice in cold water, is very tasty. Also spiced Dhobi-Wallah, raw potato sprinkled with organic salt (47p) is terrifically good value. Try it with their brown coloured sauce – they call it Aitchpi (15p). Genuine Indian atmosphere. Very thin waiters just like the supplements. Fascinating insects, exotic smells etc. Open when Dave gets out of the nick.

Theatre

Lunchtime

● Thelma Road Cafe, Gunnersbury Park. Untitled Agitprop Theatre in the Cafe.

Untitled Agitprop Theatre in the Cafe formulates a devastating indictment of commercial exploitation as applied to the context situation of the twilight urban ghettoes. As in Rhandi Jay's Ethos Vibrations, the central figure is a cafe proprietor in Gunnersbury who is anxious to close his cafe in order to go to the Betting Shop in order to back the favourite in the half past two race. The man says nothing throughout, but he listens to Radio One, whose meaningless gibberish acts as a cogent counterpoint to his oblique cigarette-smoking, sandwich rearrangement and Beckett-like cough. (Arnold Narg.)

Books

● The Day of the Eel (Gemini Press, 40p). Husband and wife research team Drs. Maurice and Doris Norris elaborate their now famous theory that eels were at one time, millions of years ago, highly sophisticated creatures organised in an underwater society of fantastic complexity including computers and laser beam surgery. Highly convincing and fascinating book.

● Down With The Fascist Pigs, by Ivy Scruggs. (Bombadil Books, 40p).
In the last few weeks, Ivy's struggle on behalf of thousands of oppressed Kleenaphone ladies has catapulted her right into the forefront of the Guardian women's page. Now Ivy tells her long-awaited story, in her own deeply unique style. She totally ridicules the whole bourgeois concept of the glamour of working class life in Neasden, where she grew up, and the degradation of women being forced to clean millions of male-chauvinist telephones every day. (Bob Haldeman).

Film Clubs

● One of Holland's least known film makers is Jan van der Ungoed Jarvis. His latest film will be shown at the George V Memorial Hall Neasden (Wednesday). Ungoed Jarvis has a sight impediment which renders him totally blind thus bringing to his work an eerie sense of incoherence and mystery. In 'The Ashtray' – a title which bears no relation to the work Van der Ungoed Jarvis' lens probes deep into the depths of darkness as he had unknowingly filmed at night-time. The knowledge by the spectator that the unchanging black screen is the result of a blind man mistakenly filming under the impression that it is daylight added to which the subject of the film is an empty blackboard painted white creates an unresolvable paradox like the problem of Binary Co-ordinates in Maths (192 minutes. Black and white).

Gay Jumble Sale

● Hope-Wallace Hall, Islington, Sat. 3 o'clock in aid of Equality for Gay Ironmongers. A really terrific selection of cast-off posing pouches in various colours, skin-tight leather motor-cycle gear, boots, chaps, jackets, wigs, one large lady's evening gown in silkette vinyl (waist 48), one pair high heeled shoes, fantastic selection Moroccan post-cards, scout-master's uniform (woggle and badges missing, etc. Fairy cakes and Gay Raffle.

Second-hand newspapers

by Barbara Nutter

Because of the price of newspapers they have become incredibly expensive. You can buy new newspapers at a lot of places in London (see pp 94–194 for special guide to news vendors and agents) but only at a price. What most people are doing now is to get their newspapers second hand.

Second hand newspapers are most often found in litter bins throughout London. Obviously the bigger type of bin (such as bins in stations and airports) are more likely to contain newspapers, as the normal bus-stop type of bin is too small to take other than tabloids.

Another good place to find really good second-hand newspapers is on the underground, particularly Racing Editions, quite often with the crossword left untouched (Cont p. 94)

TOMMY VANDERG... BLUE GRASS DOG'S DILDO ALL...
THE BEAUTIFUL NOSE FLUTE ● CURLY KEVIN WARMINSTER 1 ●
THE DAME ● ... BROS ● THE HOLY FAMILY FEATURING
LITTLE LAURIE LEVIN ● MONTY MUSLIM AND HIS ELECTRIC
BLACK MAGIC ORCHESTRA ● ANDY AND STU ● TOTTENHAM
COURT RD ● RICKY GANDALFS HAREM ● THE FURGUS
CASHIN SOUND ETC.

SCREAMING ABDABS * CECIL KING'S DIARY (only appearance in this country) TEILHARD DE CHARDIN AND THE CHARDINERS * SOUNDS * FREAKS * BORES * DRUGGIES * RUBBISH * INCREDIBLE TEDIUM * 17-YEAR OLD PERSONS WITH MOUSTACHES * A Shyster Films Production released through United Money.

IN THE EXPLODING

NEASDYN GALAXY XX

ALL THE MUSICAL MAGIC OF THE NOW LEGENDARY NEASDEN POP FESTIVAL OF 1972

Longford appeals for 'Titanic Spirit'

Rain hinders Religious Festival

Vicar declares Festival open

Widow's marrow wins judges' acclaim

Police swoop on giant marrow

There was a large crowd (E. Tharg) in Trafalgar Square last Tuesday afternoon for the official opening of this year's "Let's Save Britain From All These Frightful Dirty Books And So Forth" Festival.

The Festival was declared open by Lord Longford, who told the organisers that he had never seen such a splendid turnout (E. Tharg).

"It is marvellous" he said, "to see so many young people". (E. Tharg). "But" said Lord Longford, "we must not forget the many older folk who have done so much to help to make this Festival such a splendid success." (E. Tharg Snr. no relation).

In his speech, which was frequently applauded by the large crowd (E. Tharg), Lord Longford paid particular tribute to the high standard of many of the exhibits on display.

"What we need today" he said " is the spirit of the Titanic when hundreds of people young and old joined hands and sang 'Abide With Me' as they sank to oblivion."

Also on the platform were Mr Malcolm Muggeridge who delighted the crowd with a display of vegetarianism, Mr Cliff Richard who sang his much-loved hit of yesterday, "Livin' Doll" and Mrs Mary Whitehouse who was wearing an organza flowered cloche hat in powdered "Porno Blue" and blush pink and an off the shoulder white satin cocktail dress with denim trimmings and motor cycle-style studs with matching accessories. She carried a bouquet of Stripperamas.

The Festival opened with a special float pulled by a prize herd of Friesian Cows lent by Lord Vestey, depicting Britannia (played by Lord Longford's daughter, Lady Magnesia Freelove, wearing a see-through Union Jack) menaced by the Spirit of Darkness (Oscar Beuselinck Jnr.)

Over 29p was raised at the various stalls which organisers described as a record. Police (P.C. Ned Strangelove, or 'The Odd Copper' as he is known) praised the friendliness and co-operation of the large crowd. (E. Tharg)

One arrest was made. (E. Tharg)

THE MAN BEHIND THE LIBERAL REVIVAL
An EYE profile

Hetherington West, Newport Pagnell, Neasden-under-Lyne, Barnetson-on-Tweed - the list of feathers in the Liberal cap looks like more than just a flash in the pan. Make no mistake about it! British politics can never be the same again.

But this new Liberal Revival is no mere nine-day wonder.

It is the result of ten days' careful planning and strenuous effort by one man - "Mr. Liberal Revival" himself, Dr. Trevor Spart.

Dr. Spart, 59, is a part-time VAT consultant, who lives in an ordinary semi in the unassuming Salford suburb of Bryan's-Lapping. He is the father of Dave Spart, the outspoken young student leader, whose contributions to the underground press are regularly read by an estimated audience of Dr. and Mrs. Spart.

It was Trevor Spart who, one night two years ago, suddenly dreamed up the brilliant catch-phrase that was to sweep the Liberals to power - "Vote Liberal". "The idea just came to me in a flash" he said. "I was out drinking with some friends, when suddenly I thought that if I was a Liberal, the slogan ' Vote Liberal ' would be a great gimmick - simple, memorable, tremendous impact, and completely new."

Spart of Something Big

Spart, 62, was also responsible for the key-phrase "environmental activism", which has been the secret of the Liberals'

astonishing rise to power.

Just what does "environmental activism" mean? Explains Spart: "It means getting onto your local council, so that you can get things done - like having your drains cleaned, and finding someone to baby-sit when you want to go and see *The Clockwork Orange*.

"People means people" says Spart passionately. "What we stand for is getting instant feedback from the grassroots. At the moment people are totally alienated from the whole power-base which orientates the structurisation of society. If we are to get through to the ordinary man and woman at all levels of society, we have to try to create a sense of participation in a meaningful process of dialogue."

Dr. Spart is 83.

Hullo again! *with BAMBER GASKET*

I was driving through Esher on my way to Bletchley via the B6075 Morpeth-Baldock Ringway when suddenly I found my way barried by eight sturdy bollards and a "Pedestrians Only" sign where nought had been before. (Luckily I was able to apply my servo-assisted brakes just in time to avoid very severe damage to my near-side wing and bulkhead assembly). It seems in these days that more and more often the roving motorist, out for a casual spin, is being denied his rightful access to ancient free-ways and through-roads which for ages past have afforded great enjoyment to legions of dedicated motorists on pleasure bent. It will be a sad day indeed if these traditional thoroughfares are allowed to lapse into mere pedestrian precincts and the friendly roar that follows the accelerator pedal as it is rammed onto the floor-boards is heard no more.

As Old Jowett has it:

O to be a motorist
O'er England's many roads.

(Stevenage General Infirmary Casualty Department, Tues.)

Hell

a special report

A Message from the Chief Executive

It is a very great pleasure for me to have been invited to introduce this special supplement. The Times has always had a very special place in the hearts and minds of our people, and we are delighted to have this opportunity to present to readers of this great newspaper an objective picture of recent trends and developments 'down here'.

I feel sure that these reports can do nothing but provide a greater awareness of the tremendous achievements of recent years, and our well-founded hopes for the future. And I look forward personally to meeting even more of your readers in years to come, as guests of our great and flourishing organisation.

Old Nick

H.R.H. THE PRINCE OF DARKNESS, HADES.

PROFILE

A Leader for Tomorrow

This year marks the 2,000, 000th anniversary of the reign of Satan I, Imperial Grand-Denizen of the Nether Regions.

During the long period of his reign,'Old Nick', as he has long been affectionately known to his subjects, has shown an admirable willingness to adapt to the changing conditions of each new age, as it has arisen.

Today his reputation has never been higher, as one of the most dynamic and forceful personalities on the world stage.

Without doubt his greatest achievement in recent years has been the fostering of a growing detente between himself and the clergy.

Once implacably divided, and seemingly bent on mutual destruction, the two great powers, under 'Old Nick's' beguiling diplomacy, have moved closer together on a very wide variety of topics.

The Prince of Darkness lives a surprisingly quiet and frugal life, although he has never sought to impose his own somewhat ascetic life style on his followers. With his distinguished silvery horns, and well-groomed goatee beard (his resemblance to Sir Basil Spence has been frequently remarked upon), there is no doubt that the Devil remains the one stable element in a rapidly changing world.

Goodbye to Brimstone

by OUR INDUSTRIAL STAFF

Hell has always been rich in basic raw materials, and industry was well-established many millenia ago. A certain amount of concern has been expressed recently at predictions that natural resources of brimstone, sulphur and pitch could well be exhausted by the year 2,000,000. But Hellish scientists are quick to dismiss such prophecies as mere hysterical wishful thinking. They point to the astonishing technological advances which have been made in recent years as an indication that Hell's basic industries can look to the future with unprecedented confidence. Many new processes have been discovered which should ensure that productivity will continue to rise well into Phase Three of Eternity. The old 'brimstone method' of inflicting maximum agony, for example, is increasingly giving way to the use of napalm. Again, the primitive 'prod and poke' factories in which inmates were 'treated' by hand with forks and bludgeons have been almost universally replaced by 'electric massage parlours' and laboratories equipped with all the latest gadgetry of modern science.

tonishing growth record? Undoubtedly the advent on earth of a more relaxed attitude to inter-personal relationships and the redefining of outmoded moral guidelines has helped enormously.

Recent events in the American market, such as the adoption as official policy of stealing, lying and bribery, have been greeted here with cautious optimism. Although it is pointed out that, so far, no connection has been es-

tablished between the White House and the mass sex-killing in Texas.

Events in Britain too have been officially welcomed.

The Lambton-Jellicoe affair, the Poulson case, the refusal of the West Indies cricket team to accept an umpire's decision, have all been severally accepted as symptoms of a widespread collapse in traditional ethical values, and future developments are awaited with eager anticipation.

It's boom time for bottomless pits

by ECONOMICS EDITOR SALTPETER JAY

Never before has the Netherworld's future looked so rosy. This year the number of new immigrants has again reached an all-time record. More furnaces have been constructed in the past six months than in any corresponding period since records were kept.

Employment figures among skilled and semi-skilled imps have once again touched a new high.

What lies behind this ast-

TOURISM

Old blends with new in modern hell

The visitor to Hell is at once struck by its fascinating blend of bygone tradition and all the up-to-date trappings of the contemporary world.

A must for every tourist or businessman (two categories particularly prominent in all parts of hell) is the famous Inferno Gate of the 14th century, with its celebrated inscription. "Lasciate ogni speranze, voe ch'entrate (*or "No U Turns or Parking on Hard Shoulder"*).

The gate opens on a scene which could still in many respects familiar to Dante — as millions of folk of all nationalities jostle past each other in the narrow streets and alleys of 'Old Hell', now a pedestrian precinct. On the side of the streets, many of Hell's familiar old handicrafts are open to view. The nostalgic smell of roasted flesh wafts from many a dim doorway. The groans and excited babbling of the damned mingle with the hiss of scalded limbs, and the squeaking of ancient racks and thumbscrews (often priceless examples of old craftsmanship in themselves). But beyond the older parts of Hell, one soon comes face to face with 'the new City' - with its gleaming tower blocks, 24-lane motorways and the constant roar of a stream of

Jumbo Jets overhead, bringing in new arrivals.

Here one is transported to a new world. You may, for instance, choose to put up at The Paradise Lost Milton, with its architecture inspired by Richard Seifert, and 12-channel Muzak in every room. Or you can spend a delightful three or four hundred thousand years in the cabaret of 'the Cambodia Room', watching your nearest and dearest being blown to pieces by B-52's, to a full stroboscopic, hard-rock audio-visual accompaniment.

Critics have in the past sometimes remarked that one of the disadvantages of Hell, compared with say the Costa Brava, is that once you are there, you can never leave. But faced with this kaleidoscopic array of temptations and diversions, what sensible tourist would ever want to come back to earth?

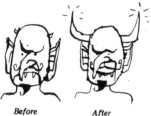

The Pleasures of Life

TODAY WE LAUNCH A SERIES BY WELL-KNOWN WRITERS ON THINGS THEY KNOW NOTHING ABOUT, BUT KNOW WHAT THEY LIKE. IN THE FIRST OF THE SERIES KINGSLEY AMIS TALKS ABOUT:

1. My Hundred Best Tunes

Kingsley Amis

Perhaps I ought to begin. *piano nobile* as they say in the trade. by admitting that I don't really know the first thing about classical music. Never mind. I'm always game for a crack at anything. particularly if there's a spot of loot at the end of the tunnel-- so here goes.

Perhaps I'd better begin by admitting that I've got a blind spot as far as old Bach is concerned. I could never get onto his wavelength. All that tinkly stuff. flutes, harpsichords and so forth.

Now. W.G. Bach. there's another bowl of soup altogether. A bit of all right. what? I know he's a big hit nowadays, but I can remember discovering him thirty years ago. Oh. another double please. old boy. Cheers! Now. where was I? Oh yes. old Ludwig van B. Bit of an old bore. to my mind. All that thumping great German soul. Give me Vivaldi any day of the week. Now there's someone who can write a catchy tune you can whistle in the bath. Oh. I'm terribly sorry. old man. I seem to

have come out without my wallet. You couldn't possibly see your way...oh, that's awfully decent of you, same again, if that's o.k........ Isn't that Ron Hall over there talking to old Bob Conquest? ...

Do you know the one that goes Rum-rum-ta-ta-teedle-eedle-too.... something like that anyway...I've always thought that was a thumping good number...It's old Wolfgang. isn't it? Cheers! I'm always getting into trouble about something I once put into one of my books. I had this character, a kind of boozy old novelist in a pub who was always scrounging drinks and writing articles about things he didn't know anything about in the Sunday papers... Anyway, he was always going round saying "Bloody Mozart", and what he really meant was "Bloody Mary"...kind of drink, y'know...yesh. I'd love one... Vodka, ther'sh a great composher for you. Do you know hish Newsh of the World Symphony ... Dit-dit-dum-da-da-dum-di-duddle-da.... (cont. Saloon Bar 94)

WE pRoMISE £1,uuu FoR

That is the astonishing offer made to any man who pays a tiny weekly premium* on a Charterhouse Oxford Norwich Union & Gnome unique hospital protection insurance scheme.

Just think of it. Only a modest outlet brings you literally thousands of pounds tax free as soon as you die.

*   £500 per week

The worst day in any man's life is when he dies. This can happen quite often without warning and the deceased finds himself unexpectedly deprived of all his possessions.

That's where Gnome's CONU scheme becomes your guardian angel. For he will guarantee you £1,000 for every day you are dead.

Let CONU bring you a trouble free

terminal experience

G.P

EVERY DAY YOU ARE DEAD

Are you worried that you may die in agony in a National Health hospital?

Our polls show over 9 out of 10 people dread the prospect of spending their last days in an ordinary NHS hospital.

THESE ARE THE FACTS AS PROVED SCIENTIFICALLY BY OUR HIGHLY TRAINED MARKET RESEARCH TEAM

1 OVERCROWDED WARDS. In 94% of NHS hospitals patients are forced to sleep eight in a bed.

2 CHRONIC SHORTAGE OF HOSPITAL STAFF. In 1973 no less than 80 operations in 100 were carried out by the patient himself. Operations ranged from advanced brain surgery to amputation of limbs.

3 IMMIGRANT DOCTORS. Figures published by the BMUJA show that 98% of NHS doctors cannot speak English and lack any professional qualifications. Literally thousands of them suffer from chronic pigmentation of the skin.

4 MEDICAL EXPERIMENTATION. The highly confidential Ponderax Report published for the BMD last year by an expert team of doctors headed by Dr. Ephraim Ponderax ASLEF, BUPA, VD revealed that 92% of NHS patients can expect to be used as "guinea pigs" once it is known that they are about to undergo a terminal experience.

Simply complete this enrolment form. You make no*** commitment of any kind.

VERY SMALL PRINT

IMPORTANT 1: Monies accrued from a weekly investment are payable only to the deceased AFTER his demise. At no stage prior or subsequent to death will dependants or relatives benefit. Only the dead man can claim.
2. The deceased must claim in person within a week of his death. Failure to do so will automatically result in confiscation of any assets which may be owing to him.

*** This word is not applicable in this sentence.

Don't let it happen to you

For only a tiny weekly outlay** you can ensure that you and your loved ones undergo a terminal experience which will be something that you will remember for the rest of your life.

★ Private rooms fitted with the very latest equipment

★ Highly skilled patrial consultants with reassuring horn-rimmed glasses and silvery-grey Doctor-style hair.

★ All the comfort of a Five Star hotel plus the very finest that 20th century Medical Science can give.

** £1000 per week

Guarantee

The Charterhouse Oxford Norwich Union & Gnome guarantees to fulfill any obligation which may be incurred as a result of any monies hereby withstanding.

Ephraim B. Ponderax
Medical Adviser

I would like to enrol as an investor in the CONU scheme.

NAME: _____
ADDRESS: _____
BANKERS CARD NO: _____

Upper Crusties

TODAY AT 10.30 a.m.
IMPORTANT OLD MASTERS. The
properties of the Master of Eigg, the Hon.
Gavin Fruit, Mr John Poulson, Mr Simon
Dee, the Earl of Gowrie, Mr Robert
Maxwell and others. Including works by
Grotti, Clarkini, the Master of Eigg,
L.F.Gunge the Younger, Turner of Neasden,
a group of important nude studies by
Guccione, and an unusual drawing by
Franz Andnebers. Catalogue (I plate)
£5.99 plus postage.

WEDNESDAY AT 11.55 a.m.

HIGHLY IMPORTANT ENGLISH AND
FOREIGN RUGS, DOORMATS AND LINOS..
The Properties of the Earl of Bethell, the
Rt. Hon. Reginald Maudling, Mrs H.D.F.
Creighton and others. Including the finest
grade of Ferguskashin, Aldatjaz, Gorblimi,
Verinaisbargin, Teluwot, Aigivitawai,
Hurrihurri, Weilstokszlazt and other lovely
weaves. Catalogue 5p.

THURSDAY AT 8.00.a.m.

THE CELLAR OF THE BRITISH
RESTAURANT, TESCO ROAD, NEASDEN.
The Property of the Official Receiver.
Including cases of important locally-bottled
Carafe wines, a rare bottle of 1903
Sandeman's Port-style Old Ruby, and a
Jumbo of "Auld Ghillie's Breeks" Hong Kong
bottled 100 per cent proof Colin Welch's
Liqueur "A wee drappie doon the gullet'll
burn your guts awa'!" Catalogue from
Slashprice Winemart Ltd., Shepherd's
Bush.

FRIDAY AT 11.00.p.m.

IMPORTANT MANUSCRIPTS, BOOKS AND
AUTOGRAPH LETTERS. The Properties of
the Pimlico Public Library, Sir Basil
Spence, the Earl of Barmey, the Knight
of Longknyves, Mr Cyril Connolly, Mr
Christopher Logue, Mr Anthony Haden-
Guest, and Steptoe and Son Ltd., Pulp
Merchants. Including the *Gesta Bororum
1522, Grammet on Death, The Moths of the
Outer Hebrides 1881, A History of the 49
Bus Route* (very rare), *The Gentleman's
Friend* (some issues missing) 1834-1860,
and letters from E.B.Smilby, Grout,
Bottinger, Hotchkiss, Smith and Others.
Catalogue 5p.

SATURDAY (Early Closing).

OBJECTS OF VERTU AND ITEMS OF
MISCELLANEOUS IMPORTANCE. The
Properties of the Dowager Lady Norman
St.John Stevas, Lord Max Roger de
Frequently, and Others. Two old shoes,
believed to have been the property of the
late Mrs Eartha Crump, a pair of dentures,
hand-painted umbrella stand by Robinson,
feathers, a pair of badgers stuffed and
mounted in an unusual position, and a very
important old mattress.

The Life of Dr. JONATHAN

BEING AN ACCOUNT OF THE LIFE AND TIMES OF THE
CELEBRATED DR JONATHAN MILLER
By his devoted friend and companion John Boswells, Gent of the Realm.

Few people in these changed times are aware that, many years ago, in the headstrong days of his youth, the great Doctor Jonathan for a while forsook the pursuit of philosophy and Science, and became a travelling player. The circumstances of this strange interlude in the great Doctor's career have become mercifully veiled by the mists of time. Nonetheless, from my investigations, I can assert that circa Anno 1960, the Doctor, being cast into indigence, fell in with a company of the acting profession, pantaloons, lewd clowns and the like. How curious a spectacle to envisage - the most elevated intellect of our age, caparisoned like a harlequin, and playing at dumb-show for the giggles of a sweaty mob, swept up from the stinking courts and rookeries of Auld Reekie![1] A twelvemonth later, it seems, the troupe came to London, and for some years they were one of the sights of Drury Lane, where their fooling was witnessed by many persons of rank and position, including, I am told, Her Majesty the Queen, and her Chief Minister, Harold Macmillan, Gent of the Realm.

---

1. *"Beyond the Fringe" to which Mr Boswells here refers was first performed in Edinburgh (Ed.)*

2. *Scotch whiskey.*

I am reminded of these curious and now little-known events by the return to the London stage of two of the great Doctor's former low companions, by name Mr Dud Moore and Sir Peter Coke, Bart. But this vulgar entertainment of theirs can be considered of little worth, now that these poor clowns must caper and jest without the assistance of that great Luminary who was formerly their presiding Genius!

Indeed, how different are their circumstances now, as the Doctor has bent himself to those Noble and Generous Pursuits for which he is rightly famed throughout all the world - viz the enlightenment of the human race on all topicks under the sun. It was engaged on such an enquiry for the improvement of mankind, that I discovered the great Doctor, when I called upon him at his well-appointed lodgings in Glos.Crescent last week.

The Doctor was seated amidst a vast throng of importunate savants. These charlatans were holding out to him pieces of card, upon which were inscribed strange hieroglyphics and devices, namely circles, wavy lines, squares and the like.

BOSWELLS: (smiling) **Pray, Sir, what means this Academy of Geometers?**

DR JONATHAN: *(smiling)* Why, Sir, these men are Fanaticks, who would persuade me that there exists some Metaphysical Phenomenon which they call 'telepathy' - whereby it is possible for one man to decipher the mind of another, without any articulation of speech. No more preposterous fancy could ever be conceived.

BOSWELLS: Sir, I have heard tell of such occurrences in the wilder regions of my native Scotland.

JONATHAN: Fie, Sir, you speak only of vile superstitious Scotchmen, whose faculties have been intoxicated by the imbibing of usquebaugh.[2] Such vain babblings are contrary to all Science, as I shall demonstrate.

At this the savants clustered round eagerly to witness the great Doctor's experiment.

DR JONATHAN: Sir, I shall now conceive a thought and meditate upon it, and you shall tell me what I am thinking. I shall give you ten minutes.

At this a rapt silence fell over the company. In the midst of us, the Doctor sat, his huge head in his hands and a contented smile upon his face.

BOSWELLS: *(after ten seconds)* Sir, I believe I am now possessed of the burden of your thoughts.

DR JONATHAN: *(playfully)* Why, Sir, what is it then? Enlighten us.

BOSWELLS: Sir, you are thinking that there is only one sage in all the world who knows everything that there is to be known - to wit, yourself.

DR JONATHAN: *(leaping from his chair in astonishment)* Gentlemen, I proffer my apologies to you all. This person has just uttered the very thoughts that were in my head. This is indeed a most remarkable addition to the sum of Scientific knowledge, and I recommend that henceforward it be known as Dr Jonathan's Extra Sensory Perception.

Two

I was lately petitioned by a young person, of most delicate address, to furnish her with privy intelligence concerning that great luminary of our age, and my good friend, Dr JONATHAN. It appeared that the young lady was presently employed on behalf of the *NEW STATESMAN,* that most estimable sheet in which the disquisitions of the good Doctor upon a wide diversity of topicks, have frequently appeared.

Now the same journal is to publish an 'in-depth profile' of the great Doctor, setting before the public his character and achievements in all their many aspects.

Coming across my friend in the congenial environs of the BBC Hospitality Room, I at once congratulated him on the honour that the *New Statesman* had accorded him.

DR JONATHAN: (smiling) Sir, this is alas a foolish enterprise of which you speak.

BOSWELLS: Why, sir, you cannot gainsay the high honour which is being paid you?

DR JONATHAN: Sir, your folly never ceases to amaze me. What mere uninformed scribbler could hope to do justice to the myriad facets of my genius? Why, there is only one person alive today whose powers are sufficient to chronicle my achievements in the realms of science, literature, medicine, the arts and the pathology of humour.

BOSWELLS: Thank you, sir, you are most kind.

DR JONATHAN: (angry) Dunderhead! Idiot!

PROF DWORKIN: Talking of the *New Statesman* reminds me that this week's issue contains a fascinating advertisement for my forthcoming dialogue on TV, concerning the current malaise which afflicts the body politic of the U.S.A. These promises to provide one of the most illuminating analyses.....

DR JONATHAN : Be silent, sir. You have presumed upon us for too long. Besides, I would recommend to you the programme in which I myself am advertised shortly to participate – to wit a debate upon the deeper significance of *Monty Python's Flying Circus*, as it reflects the alienation of contemporary mankind. I venture to suggest that no programme of the coming months will offer such rich matter, both for instruction and edification.

MISTRESS TWEEDIE: Pig!

Three

For these many months past, there has been great curiosity in all parts of the kingdom concerning the circumstances of the most celebrated mind of our age.

On Friday last, being the 6th day of October, it was therefore with the utmost joy that, upon application to that most prodigal cornucopia of wisdom and diversion – namely Mr Marconi's most excellent device, called vulgarly 'the wireless' – I heard the familiar vigorous utterance of no less than my dear friend, whom I had almost thought departed from us forever.

All at once the enigma of the Doctor's strange disappearance was made clear to all his devoted admirers. For these many months, it appeared, he has been privily removed into an attic room, far from common intercourse, there compiling many huge tomes for the publick edification, concerning divers topicks too awful and profound to bear thinking of.

The first of these mighty volumes was now subscribed, written, and fresh disbursed from the press of that friend to all poor scribes and scholars, SIR GEO WEIDENFELD.

At once, I sought out the house of my long-lost companion and mentor in Glos. Crescent, there to repair the dishevelled threads of our friendship. I discovered the great Doctor, seated among a convivial throng, including Mr Geo. MELLY, Prof. DWORKIN and Prof. AYER, the noted logician.

BOSWELLS: Pray, Doctor, acquaint us with the nature of this work lately brought to sale.

DR JONATHAN: Sir, I have endeavoured to set before the public eye, an account, never before written, of one of the most learned and philosophical figures in the history of our times. I speak of a man who not only enjoys a rare cognisance of the Mysteries of the human mind, but is also an example of something unique in our times – the power to discourse with knowledge upon topicks drawn from the kingdoms of both Art and Science. Furthermore this inestimable polymath has furnished the world with some most excellent disquisitions upon sundry other matters viz. The Pathology of Laughter, and other blessings on the human race too numerous to mention.

BOSWELLS: Then, Sir, you have, I see,

been engaged upon the practice of auto-biography!

DR JONATHAN *(angry):* Scotch porridge bag!

Prof. AYER: Why, Sir, the Doctor is referring to Dr Sigmund Freud the celebrated sage of Vienna, concerning whom he has lately invited sundry scholars to discourse most learnedly within the pages of a book.

It then fell to Prof. R. DWORKIN, the noted jurisprudent and wit, lately shipped from the plantations, to hold forth for the space of some hours upon what he described as "Freud's seminal influence on our times". Whereat the company was lulled by the Professor's words into the most exquisite slumber.

London Giants clash in Cup Draw

By E.I.ADDIO
Our Man in the Directors' Box with the Black Coffee and the Alka Seltzer.

"This one suits us fine" said a tight-lipped Ron Knee, 59, last night on learning that Neasden F.C. were drawn against Dollis Hill in the First Round of the Ringway Box Charity Trophy Cup.

Says Knee, 59: "Make no mistake. From the way we're playing lately, the Wembley towers are just around the corner."

Tight Corner Kick

But a victory over Dollis Hill will need more than just optimism on behalf of Neasden's traditionally a shen-faced supremo.

SHOCK NO. 1. Records show that in their long history Neasden have never once scored a goal, let alone beaten Dollis Hill.

Even in 1945 when the Hill were hacked down to three players, the score line from the Bridge still showed the Dollis dynamos winners by a hatful of goals.

SHOCK NO. 2. Neasden's net finders are unsettled by their poor form in recent weeks.
O'Relli has been on and off the transfer books as many times as egg, chips and beans have been on and off the menu at Drogheda's Cheery Cafe opposite the Stadium.

Disaster

Striker 'Wee Jock' Carter-Ruck has been sitting on the touchlines since Christmas nursing a broken neck.

Custodian of the uprights Wally Foot, Neasden's one-legged keeper is understood to be unavailable for the vital tie, due to his detention pending bail at the Tesco Road Police Station.

Foot, 54, the former Hainault shot-saver, was held by police at the Nat West bank (Pricerite Rd) during a 'hold-up' incident in which it was alleged he had demanded money with menaces.

Final Whistle

But perhaps the biggest set-back of all for a Neasden side dogged by disaster is that fans (Sid and Doris Bonkers) may not be on the terraces on the great day to give their support.

The mass singing by Sid and Doris of the famous chant 'Go on punch him in the face' has become an integral feature of this North Circular Derby.

But thanks to the decision by Neasden Chairman local launderama magnate Brig 'Buffy' Cohen to restyle the famous 'Waste Tip' Terraces by building an interlocking network of offices, hotels, conference centres and marinas there will be nowhere for Sid and Doris to stand.

My personal prediction is that Neasden will be lucky to lose by just the odd goal.

LATE SCORE

Inner Ringway Box Trophy Cup
(1st Round)

DOLLIS HILL....12 NEASDEN......0

(Halftime 7-0)
(Gillroy 5 Sogat 2
Pevsner (o.g.) 5)

THE LAST SIX
The Draw

Neasden   v   Dollis Hill
Hainault Ath v   Raynes Park Rvrs
Wealdstone Wndrs
  or Pinner   v   Ongar Acdmcls

IS DEEPLY PRIVILEGED TO BE ABLE AT THIS MOMENT IN TIME TO BRING YOU

TO THE CULTURAL EXPERIENCE OF
FOR A THOUSAND YEARS

List of Titles

I–V   Documents Relating to Early Life (Birth Certificate, Etc.)
VI–X Complete School Essays
XI Speeches at the Oxford Union (Complete and Unabridged)
XI–XV   Complete University Essays
XVI   The Years of Peril 1939-45 (Complete Letters to Mother while on War Service, and Full Text of Lectures to Troops: *"The Dangers of Venereal Infection While on 48-Hour Leave at Catterick"* [1944])
XVII   The Tide Turns: 1945. Documents relating to Demobilisation
XVIII–XX   Editorials and Collected Despatches from the Church Times 1946-48
XXI   The Challenge of Post-War Conditions. Collected Election Speeches 1950-51
XXII–XXV   The Years of Plenty
Documents Relating to Mr. Heath's Period of Office as Chief Whip
XXVI New Horizon: The Challenge of Europe. Despatches from Brussels 1962-63
XXVII   Setting The Shopkeeper Free: The Challenge of Resale Price Maintenance 1964
XXVIII   A Leader Is Born: Collected Conference Speeches as Leader of Opposition 1965-69
XXIX–XXXIII The Quiet Revolution: The Challenge of the Seventies

XXXIV–XL At A Stroke: A Study of Coronary Disorders in the Middle-Aged Executive by "A Doctor"
XLI–XLIV   The Twilight Years: Memoirs, as Told to Douglas Hurd and Donny Osmond ⌀

THE COLLECTED
WORKS OF EDWARD
HEATH

I enclose my cheque for £1,279 as down payment for the first of my 50 volumes of The Collected Grocer. I understand that the remaining volumes will be sent as soon as we have collected enough money to pay the printers' bill, or by 1998, whichever is the sooner. I understand that owing to the unique nature of this offer, no money can be returned to me under any circumstances. Please make cheques payable to Lord Gnome, crossed Private A/c No.41, and send to Box 1062, Banque des Anonymes, Zurich, Switzerland.

"If the police start asking questions I shall just say that you packed your things one night and left me."

"Don't I get a peck then?"

"There's not much on the television tonight."

SPLUTTER WHEEZE GASP COUGH

'ALL FOREIGNERS ON DRUGS'

*by Our Man in Munich,
Lunchtime O'Lympiad*

The Olympic movement was rocked to its foundations last night by a series of astonishing allegations from the manager of the British Ten-Day Clay Pigeon Shooting Team, Brig.Sir Herbert Gussett, against the non-British entries for the Games.

"It has become apparent in the past few

seconds" said Sir Herbert, 96, "that these foreigners will stop at nothing to do down our British lads."

Horror

Sir Herbert, 103, claimed that all the 10,000 foreign competitors here at Munich are using 'miracle drugs' to aid their performance.

"There is no other explanation for it", he

SHOCK CLAIM BY BRITISH JUDGE

(believed to be Glentweedie Special Tartan Blend - Auld Feargus says "This wan will mak' ye run and run", Guaranteed 120% proof).

Sir Herbert, who came eighth in the One-legged Hurdles at the 1904 Shepton Mallet Flower Show, is 108.

Latest results in full

ONE-MAN POGO STICK WELTERWEIGHT RELAY
1 (Gold):Omo Fadaka (Tanzania): 2 (Silver):Carter Ruck (U.S.A.): 3 (Bronze): F.Muesli (Switzerland) 4 days, 23 hrs. 27.3 mins. New World and Olympic Reocrd. British Placing 843rd: N.Weebs.

MODERN DECAMERON (Women's Heats) 1 (Gold): Jill Tweedie (U.S.A.): 2 (Silver): Mary Kenny (Eire); 3 (Bronze): Sun Tan (Formosa). British Placing: 705th F.N. Starborgling (no relation). Also ran and ran F.Cashin (D.Sketch).

PARSIFAL (ACT ONE) SINGLE-HANDED CONDUCTOR EVENT 1 (Gold): P Boulez (France) 1 hr. 37 mins.: 2 (Silver) F.Knappertsbusch (Austria) 1 hr.56 mins; 3 (Bronze) A Toscanini (Italy) 2 hrs. 7 mins. British Placings: 184th O.Klemperer 17 hrs. 58 mins.

HANDBALL TOPLESS FENCING PAIRS (French Dressage) 14 Lovely girls, All Nationalities, Show's On Now! 1 (Gold): O.Calcutta (India); 2 (Silver): E.Ba Goorm (Burma); 3 (Bronze) Anna Bolick-Steroid (Norway). British Placing:379th: R'Badger' Hall. ("This one will Ron and Ron" F.Cashin D.Sketch).

said. "These drugs are so advanced that they cannot be detected by any method known to science. But make no mistake - these chappies are using them."

Asked what evidence he could provide to support his astonishing claim, Sir Herbert, who is due to retire in 1983, rapped: "It's as clear as daylight. These foreigners have walked away with every event in the Games. How can our boys and girls be expected to compete against this kind of thing?"

World War 111

Sir Herbert's comments led within minutes to the biggest international uproar since World War II.

Seventy-four African nations threatened to stage a mass walk-out in protest against what they described as 'the most blatant and criminal act of imperialist racialism by the running dog Gussett'.

After a seventeen-hour emergency session of the United Nations Security Council, Sir Herbert denied anything of the kind.

"I was merely talking off the top of my head" he frankly admitted. "I had been experimenting with a wonder miracle drug"

Your trains tonight

Mr Stanley Your, the Dewsbury-born welder who remains Britain's hottest hope for a place in the final of the Underwater Individual Volleyball, is starting his intensive altitude-training programme on the controversial, hitherto unclimbed South-East face of Everest tonight.

50 GLORIOUS YEARS

YEARS
1922~1972

Reith Laid In Portland Place

Queen Unveils Tomb of Unknown Listener

Historic Achievement Commemorated

RASPUTIN

CARTER RUCK SINGS

BBC RIP

by Our Broadcasting Staff RENE HALFCUTFORTH

FADE IN MUSIC WHILE YOU WORK THEME

HALFCUTFORTH: 'ello, 'ello - that's 2LO's - Do you remember it?

SIR JOHN BETJEMAN (for it is he): Gosh, oh yes, goodness me, I know I do. Wasn't it fun?

FADE IN WORKERS' PLAYTIME THEME

HALFCUTFORTH: Then came the War. Great days for Broadcasting. We all needed a sense of humour then, and who better to cheer up those long dark evenings than Reg Wimble. Remember *It's That Geezer?*

WIMBLE: I say, I say, I say (*Laughter*)

DOOR OPENS: 'ullo Guvnor! (*More laughter*)

WIMBLE: What are you doing here Mrs Foggis? (*Laughter*)

MRS FOGGIS: Blimey, 'ere's another one! (*Hysterical laughter*)

FADE IN HOUSEWIVES' CHOICE THEME

HALFCUTFORTH: But there was a serious side to the War as well. Remember Winston Churchill?

CHURCHILL: Good evening.

HALFCUTFORTH: But sports fans were not forgotten.

COMMENTATOR: And here comes Jerry - he's got the spitfire on the run - oh dear, the British boy's taking a terrible pasting - there go his wings - there goes his tail - but wait a minute, our lads aren't finished yet - Good heavens! He's pranged the Bosch, after all. That's one in the eye for Hitler. (*Laughter and applause*).

FADE IN SANDY McPHERSON AT THE THEATRE ORGAN

HALFCUTFORTH: And there was music too. They were the days of the big bands. Unforgettable names like Ron Watford and the Savoy Promenaders, Ambrose Heath and his Teatime Five, Eddie Balon and the Hot Potatoes, Jackie Neasden and the Bakerlites, Geraldo, Nabarro, Essoldo, Sid Previn and the London Symphony, Monty Prattwinkle and the Mayfair Musicmakers, Carter-Ruck's Rio Rumbarenes, the Val Ungoed-Thomas Sextette. Then there were the laughter-makers - immortals whose names are written in the pages of broadcasting history - Dickie Moonbeam in *Wotcher Cock*, Gladys Hoover and Doris Bloomers in *The Naafi Lark*, Jock Norris, Dan D. Lion and Morrie Tree in *Wizard Prang*, and of course the most loveable of them all, the man himself, Max Rotten:

ROTTEN: I say, I say (*Laughter*)

DOOR OPENS: Why it's the Colonel! (*Prolonged applause*)

COLONEL PULLTHROUGH: The usual, Mabel. (*Hysterical laughter*)

ROTTEN: Mine's a stout! (*Prolonged hysterical laughter*)

HALFCUTFORTH: And then, of course, there was the girl who kept the home fires burning in the hearts of millions of listeners - Nora Rainbow herself.

RAINBOW (*sings*) *Somewhere, sometime, there'll be a blue sky waiting, Over the White Cliffs of Dover And the lilacs will bloom down Lovers' Lane And it'll be all right some day.*

BETJEMAN: I say, isn't that a lovely song? And isn't it good poetry? Better than most of the stuff they publish nowadays. It was the work of dear old Monty Prattwinkle. No one remembers him now. But there was a time (cont. 94 metres VHF)

GREAT MOMENTS OF
1922 ——— TELEVISION ——— 1972

1~ Face to Face

UNDOUBTEDLY THE GREATEST TELEVISION SERIES OF ALL TIME WAS JOHN FREEMAN'S IMMORTAL SERIES OF FACE TO FACE INTERVIEWS. IN THESE PROGRAMMES, THE MEDIUM OF TELE-VISION GREW UP AT LAST, SHOWING ITS FULL POTENTIAL AS A VEHICLE FOR MATURE EXPRESSION AND IN-DEPTH EXPLORATION OF THE INMOST EXPER-IENCE OF THE HUMAN SPIRIT.

Freeman: Lord Reith, you are perhaps best known as the first Director-General of the BBC.

Reith: Aye, Aye. Mebbe. Mebbe.

Freeman: It must have been a tremendous challenge.

Reith: Aye. Aye. It was that. Aye etc.

Freeman: After being Director-General, you went on to become Managing Director of Imperial Airways. That must have been an enormous change.

Reith: Aye, Aye. It was. It was. Och.

Freeman: And then you left the Airways to become the head of the Commonwealth Development Corporation. That must have been a tremendous change for you, too?

Reith: Aye. It was. It was. The noo.

Freeman: Lord Reith, looking back on such a full and varied life, do you ever think that there was anything else that you would like to have done?

Reith: Aye. There are one or two things.

Freeman: What sort of things.

Reith: Och well, I would like to have been Winston Churchill. I never thought much of him. And I would like to have been the King. And God, that's a job I always thought I could have done - keep me fully stretched, ye ken. Aye, aye, but it was not to be, it was not to be. As Burns said "Ye canna win'em all".

Freeman: Lord Reith, thank you very much.

MORON SHALL SPEAK UNTO MORON

B.B.C.

"How we made 'War'"

by Mervyn de Quetteville

It was as long ago as 1972 that we first had the idea of doing *'War and Peace'* on the small screen. I was having lunch in the canteen when Dick Neabs, who is fantastically well-read, casually dropped the idea that 'War', as the unit came to call it, would make a fantastic serial, on the lines of 'Forsyte'.

"You must be joking", said Head of BBC Features Wally Fabric. "It would cost a bloody fortune."

However, to cut a long story short, when I told him we could flog it all over the world, he gave us the thumbs up.

"War" was born.

The Road to Wigan Pierre

"It was a terrific challenge", says Wigan-born Boris Hope-Wallace, who was chosen from a short-list of over 1000 actors, to play the part of Pierre - the aristocratic dropout who finally won the heart of the lovely Natasha.

Says Hope-Wallace: "There is a lot of me in Pierre. He is fantastically sensitive, and has this terrific effect on women."

"It was a terrific challenge", says casting director Terry Fick-Challenge, 23. "I looked through well over a million pictures of young girls before Lord Longford came in and told me to get on with the job of finding someone to play the part of Natasha, the spoiled upper-class flirt, who can't stop falling in love."

"I tell you, I was pretty desperate - but then a friend rang me and said 'Have you thought of Mary Whitehouse?'

"At first it seemed ridiculous - but then the whole thing suddenly came together."

"It is a terrific challenge" frankly admits vivacious tousle-haired Mary. "I see Natasha basically as a middle-class house-wife who spends her time watching television and maintaining decent standards."

All-Tzar cast

Meanwhile in a field near Raynes Park, twenty-five unemployed Albanian waiters were being carefully drilled for months to re-enact an exact replica of the Battle of Borodino.

"It was a terrific challenge", says Special Effects Executive Rick Mansworth, "getting 25 people to look like an army of two million men.

"But in the end it was dead simple. We just used a very small camera, lots of mirrors and got these blokes to run round and round the camera hundreds of times.

"I tell you the result is fantastic. It looks just like a load of 25 blokes running round the camera hundreds of times. You get to recognise them after a bit, and you begin to look out for your favourites."

These men will run and run

"It was a terrific challenge" says Brig-General 'Buffy' Frobisher (no relation), Lecturer in the History of Military Uniforms at Sandhurst.

Frobisher has seen service in many BBC programmes. He first saw action in the *Great War* series as long ago as 1964, was mentioned in the *Radio Times* for his part in Culloden, and was wounded in *The*

British Empire, when an artificial plastic limb exploded in his face during the Indian Mutiny.

"For *'War'*", says Frobisher, "I had to spend hours watching the King Vidor film to make sure that we got the uniforms exactly right. Considering that most of them will never be seen on the screen, this represents a really remarkable waste of time."

Artificial Lom

But perhaps the most remarkable achievement of all is the casting of Herbert Lom as Napoleon.

"It is uncanny" says Producer Solly Gaythorne-Hardy-Annual-Outing: "he is the spitting image of Herbert Lom in the King Vidor film. The viewers will just not be able to tell them apart."

"It is a terrific challenge", says Lom, who plays the part of the reckless Corsican upstart who risks all for the woman he loves.

"There is a lot of Napoleon in me" admits Lom, as he pours another wee dram of Special 4-star Cognac de St Emilion-Oûsewives-Yvry-Dès-Picques-À-Patînes-Oeuf-Binnes-en-Sieyes-Bignes-Mignes-Hines.

Count Tolstoy is 103.

BBC2   Thursday *tv*

8.30 *Colour: New series*

War and Peace

Trouble starts when young Napoleon Bonaparte gets mixed up in a plan to conquer the world. Meanwhile in faraway Russia, a young girl sits by a spinning wheel dreaming of the man she will one day marry. Will it be dashing young subaltern Prince Andre Previn? Or will it be bumbling bespectacled intellectual Pierre Boulez? Or will naughty Nappy's little plans upset the apple cart for all of them? Tonight's gripping instalment, which includes amazing footage of Rodney Pattisson winning the first day of the Flying Dutchman Class, takes us into some of the most agreeable corners of old St. Petersburg.

Cast in order of appearance

Natasha	VIVIEN LEIGH
Pierre	CHARLES AZNAVOUR
Old Count Bolkonsky	A.E.MATTHEWS
Old Jolyon	ISIDORE GLUCKSTEIN
Duke of Wellington	BASIL RADFORD
Napoleon	SEAN CONNERY
Nikolai Rostov	GORDON HONEYCOMBE
Ballsov	MERVYN DAVIES
Anatole Kuragin	KENNETH MORE
Count Clarkov Civilizationovitch	JACK HAWKINS
Peter Ustinov (as a young man)	TIBOR SZAMUELY
Sir Solly Zuckerman	ROBERTSON HARE
Droshky Driver	NIKOLAUS PEVSNER
Rudi	WILLIAM DAVIS
Trotsky	MEL LASKY
Rasputin	JONATHAN MILLER
Old Peasant	WILFRID HYDE-WHITE
Countess Magnesia Freelov	SABRINA
Olga Korbut	JIM NAST
Russian Army	ROGER PROTZ
French Army	NED SHERRIN AND FRIEND
Old Beuselinck	RUPERT DAVIES
Young Beuselinck	PEREGRINE WORSTHORNE
Old Peasant	DAVID KOSSOFF
Moujik	GYLES BADBRETH
Kulak	LORD VESTEY
Cossack Hordes	E.THARG

Songs: *Let's Be Volga, Siberian Serenade* and *Balalaika Gal Like You* by Arnie Goodman and Hal Hyams.

Produced by Bryan Forbeski

The Private Eye Critical Viewers

The games people play

Tonight sees the return of the award-winning series **The Muck Spreaders (10.15 ITV)** by H.E. Beetroot. Tonight's story **The Compost Heat**, set in the depths of Mangleshire in 1927, tells the tragic story of Enoch Worzel, a one-legged turnip-shredder and his unrequited love for Sally the goat. The **Sunday Debate (6.14 BBC1)** asks Whither the Permissive Society? with Reginald Maudling, Trevor Huddleston, Enoch Powell, Bernadette Devlin, John Mortimer and Jill Tweedie.

Later Richard Crossman

talks to Reginald Maudling about Enoch Powell and Jill Tweedie **(BBC1 11.15)** while in **Open Night (ITV 11.15)** Kenneth Allsop talks to Ludovic Kennedy about taking off his glasses.

And too many detectives?

A fascinating **Panorama** special **(8.00 BBC1)** looks at the future of the office-furniture industry now that Britain is in the common market. Alistair Brunette talks to Reginald Maudling about new techniques in management consultancy and there is a film-profile of Richard Crossman. **The World In Action** special—**The Poulson File (8.00 ITV)**—is a documentary about bee keeping in Northumberland.

Panel Game **Call My Agent (BBC2 8.55)** offers a chance to clapped-out old bores Frank Muir and Patrick Campbell to earn a lot of money. Chaired by chuckling Robert 'Baldy' Robinson.

Mourners on a coach-trip

Whatever you do don't on any account miss tonight's Wednesday Play **Joe Hartlepool's Last Fling**, by television's most exciting playwright today, Colin Northerner. Northerner is right back on form with this highly realistic account of a 60-year-old Rotherham rivet-

welder's mate, Stan Hornipants (sensitively portrayed by Reginald Maudling) who falls violently off a ladder onto his childhood sweetheart Violet Stringvest (a beautiful performance here by Jill Tweedie). Directed by Trevor Huddleston.

Un Homme Et Un Matelot (BBC2 Friday). Louis Malle-de-Mer's poignant exploration (1951) of the sensitive relationship between two human beings who meet on holiday in Baldock. Watch out for the famous bathroom scene and Malle-de-Mer's revolutionary use of underwater photography.

Blimey Wot a Lark! (ITV Friday). British film classic (1949) with Kenneth More, Alastair Sim and Wilfred Hyde-White as three sailors who are shipwrecked with a girl's school hockey team led by the ever-hilarious Joyce Dredfell. (See **Where's My Money? BBC2 Thursday**). Directed by Bryan Forbes.

He Wore a Yellow Ribbon (Sunday BBC2). The last in the current series of Film Classics by John Ford Maddox Brown tells the story of how a not-very talented man set out to make a series of tedious films about a man's duty to do what he's got to do which were later extravagantly overpraised by pseuds like Philip Jenkinson. (Black and white). See **Film Night.**

Guide to the week's tv

WEDNESDAY

Where the King of Spain still rules

Necrophilia is something that most people probably shy away from so all the more reason to watch Man Alive's **Some Like It Cold (BBC2 9.10)**, a gravely sensitive study of an anonymous necrophile. How can the community help people who suffer from the desire to watch this type of programme? Jeanne La Bagge talks to Reginald

Maudling about this agonising dilemma.

At 10.45, Ludicrous Kennedy takes his glasses off on **Midweek (BBC1)** in which viewers can phone in and ask a welfare officer and a qualified prison visitor if the programme could be taken off.

Meanwhile, on BBC2's **Edition (10.45)** Kenneth Allsop casts a critical eye over the world of the media. This week Ludicrous Kennedy looks at the increasing boredom of television on Wednesday nights.

THURSDAY

Brilliant return (for fiftieth time) of Ronnie Fartarse in a new series **Up Baldock!** With Ronnie at his fabulously

funniest as a Pakistani eunuch in medieval Newport Pagnell.

For music lovers, don't miss **Where's My Money? (10.15 BBC2)**, a second chance for Joyce Dredfell and Christopher Robin to take some more money.

FRIDAY

If you've got a date on Friday, cancel it and stay at home for the Dimbleby **Talk In (10.15 BBC1)** which looks at the problem of acute boredom with Reginald Maudling, Richard Crossman and Kenneth Allsop and a studio audience composed of chronic sufferers.

In **Famous Old Queens (BBC2 9.00)** Dr. Roy Strangelove gives a brilliantly

evocative satirical impersonation of Sir Kenneth Clark, with the help of a pair of glasses and a false moustache. Very naughty!

Stay up and watch **Film Night (BBC2)** for a rare glimpse of Philip Jenkinson and Joan Bakewell starring as a tousle-haired pseud and a mini-skirted trendy who go on about films no-one's ever heard of. This week the Count de Monte Prattwinkel, maker of **The Wheelbarrow** (1945) and **Bonjour, Matelot!** (1951).

SATURDAY

Open End (BBC2 6.00–1.30) has Joe Mediocre introducing guests from the world of arts, politics and entertainment. This week Reginald Maulding, playwright Colin Northerner, comedian Ronnie Fartarse,

Jill Tweedie, satirist John Wells, the Zimbabwe Parachutists Bongo Band, Frank Muir and Dennis Norden, Waldo and his Dogs of Many Nations, Kenneth Allsop and an extract from the Roundhouse production of *The Incredible Exploding Lew Grade's Fat Cigar* by Charles Horsfilm and Monty Madness.

POETRY CORNER

LINES ON THE ARRIVAL OF MR. AND MRS. GOUGH WHITLAM

Greetings, Gough Whitlam!
Incidentally your name
Is a most unusual one.

Gough! Whence does it
Come from? I have
To confess I have
Never written
A poem about
Anyone called Gough
Before.

When I asked Keith
What he knew
About Gough Whitlam
He had no idea
Who I was talking
About.

> E. J. Thribb (17)

'GRATE!'

Soccer's Naughty No.9 Shirt comes home

E.I. Addio
Our Man With the Delirium Tremens

The Soccer World was rocked to its foundations today by the shock news that former Wayward Genius Irish born Italian immigrant Bert O'Relli, 19, has begun training again at Neasden bridge stadium.

An ashen faced Ron Knee 59 told reporters: "It's great to have Bert back in the squad. His game will add a much needed impetus to the midfield where hitherto Neasden's 1-1-9 system has lacked cogency."

Penalty

Bert O'Relli promised to quit football for good at the North Circular Quarter Sessions earlier this year.

At the time he told the world's press "I quit. I will be happy never to kick a footballer again."

Strange Twist

But today, after a lay off of exactly 6 months O'Relli, looking tired and overweight is pushing himself to get back in shape in time to stop the goal-famine that has plagued this relegation-rated club all season.

But not everyone is happy with O'Relli's comeback.

One-legged Protector of the posts, Wally Foot, expressed doubts about the return of the midfield super-star. "I thought we had seen the last of this big-headed yob" he said.

"Time after time" went on the mono-limbed net-minder "we would hang about the Bridge waiting for him to turn up before the kick-off.

Knee's Den

"But quite often his psychiatrist should keep him at the clinic all afternoon thereby provoking Sid and Doris to acts of mindless violence when the park was void of action."

But Neasden's tight lipped supremo Knee today dismissed such fear as 'groundless'.

"The Club is also groundless" he said "as a result of Sid and Doris letting off a parcel bomb following last Saturday's result."

LATE SCORE

North Circular Challenge Shield (1st Round)

STANMORE ATHLETIC...12 NEASDEN...0
(Pevsner 5 o.g.,
Mahood 3,
Boothroyd 2,
Handelsman 1,
Brockbank 1)

Pitch: Bomb-cratered
Attendance: 2
Man of match: Stanmore's exciting number 3 shirt Ernie Waugh

THE UNPUBLISHABLE DIARIES OF EVELYN BAUGH

*These are just some of the sparkling, irreverent judgements on his contemporaries which dot the pages of **The Unpublishable Diaries of Evelyn Baugh**. For the next three years **Private Eye** will be publishing exclusive extracts from the most outspoken and brilliant literary memoir of our time.*

Novelist, raconteur, recluse, devout Jehovah's Witness, Baugh observed the human race with a jaundiced eye from his bed in the London Clinic, where he spent many years as a chronic victim of alcoholism, syphilis, paederastic compulsions and incontinence.

Every night, after his customary six bottles of vintage methylated spirits, Baugh would attempt to scrawl down some of his blurred impressions of the day. Often indecipherable, always illiterate, these diaries are nevertheless the very stuff of which immortal literature is made.

In order to protect the many prominent people named by Baugh, a number of loyal supporters of both political parties (led by Mr. Edward Short MP) have joined together to ensure that the reputations of innocent politicians are no longer "dragged in the mud" without a chance of reply. For instance, the name of the well-known former Tory Minister Lord Molson will be changed throughout to "Tom Driberg", in order to protect the innocent. The chief character named in the incident at the Prancing Buffalo Club, Frith Street, leading to later proceedings at the Marlborough Street Magistrates Court, will be known throughout simply as 'the Hon. D. Astor'.

The Diaries begin in 1917, when Baugh was a sixth-former at Shafting College, Sussex.

---

29 JULY. Went for walk on Downs with M*****. He told me he had sodomised with P*******. It is too too sick-making and foul, particularly since I fancy P******* myself. Driberg and I decide to tell the HeadMan.

We knock on his study door. There is a scuffling from inside. We throw open the door, switch on the light, and find the Head on the sofa, sodomising with Q******* Altogether too *degoutant*. After tea I went into the town with Smithers to throw stones at a few oiks. Very satisfying. Decide to become 7th Day Adventist.

30 JULY. St. Jocelyn's Day. Stayed in bed and got very drunk. No one to sodomise with. Everyone at cricket. Too too yawn-making.

31 JULY. Cecil (Beaton) has been expelled for running a white-slave racket. Serve him right, the little tick. Killed three oiks with empty '06 claret bottles thrown from San window. Very satisfying. Decide to become Moravian Brother.

Harold Macmillan

*"A fearful little jumped-
up publisher's son, dreadful social climber, mar-
ried above himself -
altogether too blush-
making."*

Winston Churchill

*"Drunken slob, mas-
querading as a states-
man. Smells like a
dray-horse."*

Pope John XX111

*"Typical little jumped-
up greasy wop. Can't
even speak English.
Should have been a
waiter in Soho."*

After his comparatively uneventful school-
days. Baugh went up to Oxford. Here in
the glittering world of the Gay Young Things -
including Arnold Prout, Basil "Florrie"
Meab and E.F. Bumme - many of whom
were later to die so tragically young in
the back-streets of Algeciras - Baugh was
in his element. He was enchanted by the
wit, the elegance, the insouciant sophisti-
cation of post-war Oxford. It was the time
of the famous 'aesthetes', including the
legendary Hon. Sid Beloff, who kept a pea-
cock in his rooms at Christchurch, and
once astonished a group of passing rowing
men by chanting at them through a mega-
phone Verlaine's poem "Bonjour matelots".

12 JANUARY. V. drunk since New Year's
Eve. Woken up by Claud (Cockburn),
Peter (Quennell) and K. (Clark). We go to
the pub, and drink thirteen bottles of Green
Chartreuse. K. horribly sick. We carry
him home to his rooms. Very disagreeable.

4 AUGUST. Feast of the Mortification of
the Blessed Arnold. One of Lavinia's
parties. All the usual crowd. Claud.
Peter, K., Lavinia. -- was there, whoring
shamelessly in a corner with a spotty girl

called **********. I was disgusted.
Thought of joining Plymouth Brethren.

16 SEPTEMBER. We went round to Alec
(Douglas-Home) 's rooms in Peckwater
and smashed them up. Everyone v. drunk
and sick, except myself. Horrible, disgusting, ghastly.

17 SEPTEMBER. Went up to town with
Frank (Longford), Tony (Powell), John
(Betjeman), Maurice (Bowra), Basil (Meab)
and Arthur (Askey). We went to restaurant
car where some dreary little oik refused to
give us lunch. We smashed the place up,
while Basil sodomised shamelessly in a
corner with the ticket collector. We all
got v. drunk, on claret, green chartreuse,
port and champagne. When we arrived at
Paddington we were all v. sick. Cecil got
hold of some whores in Praed Street and
we all went to The Purple Jacaranda Club
in Dean Street. Frank did very amusing
dance on top of piano, wearing Zazie's
undergarments, and sung a filthy nigger
song. I can't remember the words.
Everyone whored, sodomised and got v.
drunk. K. v. sick. We were all arrested by some dreary little policeman. Basil
agreed to sodomise with him for 10/-
and he let us off. Decide to join Russian
Orthodox Church.

The Queen

"Frightful little Hun on the make. Why they ever let these people into the country I can't think."

Evelyn Baugh

"A fearful little jumped-up publisher's son, dreadful social climber, married above himself - altogether too blush-making."

WHOUGH'S WHOUGH IN THE WHACKY WHORLD OF WHAUGH

HAROLD ACNE. Famous aesthete. A seminal influence on many of the brilliant Oxford generation of the 20's. Retired at age of 21 to famous Villa Puovi near Florence. Interested in Ming vases, Balinese temple sculptures and sailors. Books include *Some Problems in Quattrocento Byzantine Iconography*, and *Icon Give You Anything But Love, Sailor*.

ABLE-SEAMAN "NED" AKROYD. Friend of above.

LADY GERVASE DE VERE HARRINGTON-GARDENS. Youngest son of 14th Marquess of Paddington-Station. Loved cream buns.

KENNETH CLARK (later LORD CLARK). Lives at Saltwood, Kent. Famous for his impersonations of Bernard Berenson and Dame Myra Hess.

LADY CYNTHIA NYMPHOMANIAC. His brilliant parties at Droppings were famous in the 20's. Committed suicide Tristan da Cunha, 1934. Baugh was in love with him because he was in Debrett.

DEBRETT. Butler to the above.

ARNOLD GOODMAN (now LORD GOODMAN). Legal adviser to many whose names do not appear in Baugh Diaries.

JOHN WELLS. Brilliant young man about town and female impersonator. Described by Baugh as "I'm glad to say I don't think

Readers are advised to cut this out and keep it by them in case of emergency.

I've ever heard of him." Often seen at Lady Magnesia Freelove's glittering soirees.

LADY MAGNESIA FREELOVE. Well-known Catholic apologist and historian.

FATHER DE LONGFORD. Jesuit priest-about-town who regularly heard confessions in a Marseilles brothel. Died of syphilis at age of 93.

LE VICOMTE DE POUILLY DEFENSE DE FUMÉ. Cocker spaniel belonging to Griselda Badger, the actress.

JOHN DE TROP. Famous collector of Victorian tram tickets. Was rumoured to be able to recite 'The Charge of the Light Brigade' backwards in French. A lover of sailors, he once inspected the Home Fleet disguised as the Emperor of Indo-China. Died insane in 1932.

"FRED" NORRIS. Baugh's 'scout', known as 'Yobbo'. Once thrown into Mercury in mistake for the Archbishop of Canterbury.

QUEEN MARY. The famous ocean-liner. Baugh once saw her while on a croquet holiday at Ventnor. Much loved by sailors, who knew her as 'the old Queen'.

© The Widow Baugh and Hon. D. 'Nora' Astor, 1973.

NEXT WEEK: *An orgy at Ramsay Macdonald's —Baugh takes up heroin smuggling—Frank arrested for 'le vice anglais' in Dieppe—K. v. sick.*

ROW LOOMS OVER THREAT TO GUSSET COLLECTION

By Insightspectrumprobegrope Team P.B.Thard

A major row is brewing in the art world over the threatened break-up of one of the largest collections of *objets de maison,* Edwardian photographs, *choses bizarres* and other Very Important Old Things still in private hands.

The collection formed the world-famous Gussett Bequest. started in 1883 by the great-grandfather of the present trustee, Sir Herbert Gussett, C.H.

Choses on now

For some time now experts have been worried by the appearance at auctions of a number of items from the Gussett Collection. in different parts of the country.

Last July. for example. at the little Oxfordshire village of St John Stevas. a unique pair of Shoe Trees. thought to be the only ones of their type left in England. was sold to an anonymous buyer from a Pink Elephant Stall at the local Conservative fete held at the Church of England Comprehensive School.

Last night, Dr Roy Strange, the colourful recluse. said from his ormolu home in Kensington: "These Trees are irreplaceable. They are the work of the great Birmingham School of the nineteenth century, as the words 'Property of the Seaview Hotel, Newport Pagnell', chased on the ironwork, clearly show. If they were to be lost to America, it would be a national disgrace".

Tragedy

The now world-famous Gussett Collection was begun in a Dorset vicarage nearly 100 year ago. The founder was the Rev. Moishe Pitt-Weidenfeld-Gussett, a typical rural clergyman and antiquarian of his time.

He and members of his family built up the collection from their frequent travels over many years, in particular their annual expedition to Bude.

Among the early acquisitions to the now literally worthless collection were an array of late nineteenth century Shrimping Nets, Buckets, Spades and the famous 'Ilfracombe Biscuit Barrel', still containing some fragments of the original biscuits.

But what makes the collection unique is the album of more than 50 photographs, assembled by the founder's son, Col. Fitzherbert Blessington Pitt-Gussett during the Edwardian period. The photographs were shot by the then revolutionary Pitt-Fox-Strangeways Method (of which Whistler remarked in a celebrated aside: 'C'est magnifique mais ce n'est pas daguerrotype').

The photographs provide a unique record of life in Edwardian Newport Pagnell, before the arrival of the motorway.

STOP PRESS

It was revealed last night that an anonymous philanthropist (believed to be Lt Col "Buffy" Frobisher) had agreed to purchase the entire collection for the nation, for an undisclosed sum (believed to be £2.46p).

"I never wanted these pictures to go to America" said owner Sir Herbert Gussett, "even though they are slightly foxed, as indeed am I, by the fact that Buffy has coughed up such a generous donation. His splendid gesture will certainly go some way towards satisfying the demands of the Wessex Winemart Co. (Telegrams and Cables: GROTPLONK), which have made this whole tragic business so pressing".

You asked, we answer—eight important questions about Value Added Tax.

Recently people from all over the country were asked: "Do you have any questions about the introduction of Value Added Tax?" Many vital and probing issues were raised. Here are some of them—

1

"Vat's it all about, zen?"
William Davis, Dusseldorf

Andre Previn explains:
   A sense of humour is a very wonderful thing and helps make the world go round. Music, too, has the power to transport the troubled spirit into a wonderful world of tranquility. Elgar, Mozart, Norrie Paramour. These names are evocative of the eternal joys that music brings.

© Previtoons Ltd. Wardour Street.

2

"Isn't VAT a sort of whiskey?"
Mrs. D. Bethell, Newport Pagnell

Jeremy Conglosse, senior executive Conglosse Arslikker, Twytte Advertising Ltd. replies:
   Of course it's not you silly old cow! Just how daft can anyone get?
   But never mind. Because it's thanks to you that my agency gets paid millions of pounds to put together full page advertisements like this.

3

"Why do we believe in VAT?"
Rev. J.C. Flannel, Neasden

   More and more people are today discovering for themselves what a difference VAT can make in their everyday lives. VAT is everywhere — even in the supermarket and the humble butcher's shop. We are all of us part of the kingdom of VAT. If you would like to know more about VAT write to the Society for the Promotion of VAT, Montefiore House, Kingston.

4

"What is VAT all about?"
Mr. L. Burgis, Watford

Patrick Moore replies:
    At present we know really very little about Value Added Tax. But over the next few months we are hoping to piece together the vital clues which will help to answer the questions that have baffled scientists for centuries. Goodnight.

5

"How do I know if I've got VAT?"
A.B. Howard Naughty, Portsmouth

Dr. Ephraim Ponderax ASLEF BUPA says:
    There are more whory old legends about this than almost any other disease that doctors come up against. The truth of the matter is that you can get VAT anywhere. No one is immune. The main thing is to stay in bed and keep warm. That will be twelve gns. Thank you very much. No I'd rather not shake your hand. You never know where it's been do you?

6

"After months of suffering the relief is unbelievable."
Mr. Terry Trethowan, Basildon

    For years I have been a chronic sufferer from piles of money. I was told that nothing could be done to relieve the agony and shame that this condition can bring. But now thanks to new-formula VAT my piles of money have virtually disappeared.

7

Mrs. Lycett-Green, Willesden

I couldn't believe my eyes! Woollens whiter than white! Colours came out just like new. And mmm— so soft! Just the way I like them. From now on its square-deal VAT in the king-size container every Monday.

8

Mrs. Mavis Longford, Oxford

    I just found it very boring. There was nothing exciting about it at all.

INDUSTRIAL NEWS Prisoners threaten National Strike

By Our Industrial Correspondent

The National Union of Alleged Criminals Pending Appeal (NUACPA) gave warning yesterday of a national strike unless their demands were met immediately.

Speaking from the Union's HQ at Transportation House, fiery General Secretary "Slasher" Gathorne-Hardy outlined the five-point peace plan which he claimed could bring an end to strife-torn prison land.

1. Let us all out.
2. Give us a chance to have a look around.
3. Let us back in again, if we don't like the look of it.

MAXIMUM SECURITIES

A slashen-faced Gathorne-Hardy, 59, said "I speak from deep conviction (8 years for GBH etc.) My men do a 24-hour-a-day, seven-day week job in conditions of considerable discomfort, which most people would not be prepared to do.

"Let's face it, we provide a valuable social service. As prisoners we have waived our rights to maim, rape, burgle and murder ordinary members of the British public especially the very young and the very old, so that people can sleep peacefully in their beds at night".

DAYLIGHT ROBBERY

A spokesman for the confederation of British Prison Governors said: "I am only too willing to sit down at the wire netting and thrash things out in an uncivilised manner.

"Of course prisoners have their grievances like anyone else and I think in all fairness they should be given a fair crack of the whip."

" . . . Well that's about it, Sam. Hope Angela and the children are in good shape. All the best . . . "

"Anything on it, sir?"

Your guide to VAT

Our experts answer your queries

● *Dear Doctor Wendy,*

Am I more likely to become pregnant as a result of this continental tax?

WORRIED -Ongar

William Davis Writes:

Dear Worried,

VAT a question I ask you. Geddit?

W.D.

● *Will I pay more for my pornography?*

Lord Longford
Soho

Peter Jay comments:

This is a hard one. You may get a slight rise in some shops.

● *Given the basic infrastructure per pro investment durables, can we expect an across-the-board fluctuation of pro rata exchange bondage due to VAT standard at-source deductions as and when existing tariff multiples are seasonally adjusted in accordance with fixed-parity monetary norms, or to put it simply, will the recessionary trends prevalent as a result of the Berne agreement conversely lead to a falling off of long-term per capita GNP?*

Arnold Wesker.

Samuel Brittan says:

Yes.

As the Great Debate about Pornography continues, we bring you

THIS FANTASTIC OFFER!

THE LORD GNOME

PORNOBORE BOOK CLUB

Every volume in this superlative collection

is printed on super-sensitive gossamer style Gnomex and scientifically wrapped to ensure maximum safety.

GUARANTEED not to interfere with your pleasure.

A library of distinction and discrimination

Each month, hundreds of new books about pornography are published. Today more than ever, it is the duty of every aware person to keep abreast of the latest thinking in this controversial field.

As more and more books pour from the presses, it becomes harder and harder to keep up with the newest trends.

But now you can sit back and let our hand-picked team of experts choose for you, month by month, the most boring book about pornography published in the previous weeks.

These are the men who will choose your Pornobore Selection:

✶A.J.P Taylor, world-famous historian, and author of the best-selling *Beaverbore*. As seen on TV.

✶Professor Raymond Williams, author of *The Boring Revolution, Culture and Boredom* and many other works on the subject.

✶ Lord Clark of Civilisation, world-famous connoisseur, and author of *The Bore, The Life and Times of Bornard Borenson* etc.

This Month's choice

PORNOGRAPHY The Case In Favour. A symposium with contributions by John Mortimer, Gyles Badbreth, Mr Lucky Maltezer (Proprietor of 'Norteeboox', Filth Street, Soho) and Mr Barry Fantoni, Apostolic Delegate to the First Church of Christ Sensualist. Edited by Prof. R. Dworkin, Regius Professor of Jurisprudence at the University of the Freddie Ayer.

PORNOGRAPHY The Worm in the Bud. A psycho-sexual enquiry into deviationist patterns in contemporary society, ed. by David Holbrook, with an introduction by David Holbrook. Contributors inc. David Holbrook (originally published by Holbrooks Ltd., Holbrook Farm, Holbrook, Devon.)

POETRY CORNER

LINES ON THE VISIT TO BRITAIN OF THE DALAI LAMA

Hello, Dalai!
(No disrespect
Intended) You are
Here from the
Mysterious
Country on the
Roof of the World
About which so
Little is known
Even now.

You are a great
Spiritual leader
With your bald
Head and sari.
To hundreds of
People in your
Native Tibet
You are God
Incarnate.

Dalai Lama.
The name itself
Is strange.
Keith's mum however
Confused you with
The Abominable Snowman.

E.J.Thribb (17)

GASKET'S RURAL RIDES

Blandford to Bude

May 9. I set off early today in order to catch the rush hour jams and at approximately 0937 drew in to the Hoxted Services Area just off the Morpeth Orbital Ringway. This is a most pleasant services area affording the motorist a choice of no less than eight different brands of juice and a wonderfully efficient Wile-U-Wate wheel-balancing and silencer service. I left the old wagon with a Mr. Turgis and tooled over to the Leisurama Mini-Mart where I purchased a roll of polos, twenty Passing Cloud, a box of matches, a packet of Handy Andies, some lighter fuel and a copy of the *Daily Express*.

Happily ensconced in the Eric Morley lounge which has a marvellous view looking over miles of unspoilt motorway, I opened the paper only to read of yet another case of a party of motorists lost on Spaghetti junction.

It seems incredible to me that we allow people like this on the roads. Apparently a Mr. and Mrs. Baxter from Salford along with Mrs. Baxter's neighbour Mrs. Spooner and her mother had set out "just for a

spin" - I am quoting from the *Express* story - and were last heard of approaching Spaghetti from the Bromsgrove Flyover. After that - nothing.

I wonder when people will realise that this kind of journey is not for amateurs. Even hardened professional motorists like myself find 'Old Spag' a treacherous place to be at the best of times. There are a hundred and one spots where if you take a wrong turning you can find yourself miles from anywhere beyond rescue. I know every inch of Spag blindfold but even *I* make sure that I go well prepared. But these people seem to have gone out in their carpet slippers, with no map or charts of any kind, no compass or flares - and to top it all - just one packet of toffees between the four of them.

I know it's too late now for the lost Hillman Huskie and its occupants. But you may be sure there will be others. To these people - take a tip from Gasket: Stick to the B roads and leave the big stuff to the Pros.   (Gatwick By-Pass)

THE Sun

FORWARD WITH THE PEOPLE   3p   Wednesday, April 11, 1973

MILLIONAIRE SEX FIEND DIES IN S. OF FRANCE LOVE NEST

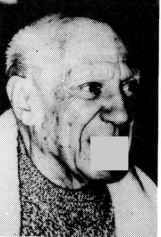

By SUN REPORTERS   Canned, Tuesday

They called him "El Sexy" in this sun drenched, white-washed paradise they call 'Sex-en-Provence'.

Throughout his 91 years he just couldn't keep his eyes - or his hands - off 'les dames'.

His women came in all shapes and sizes - lissom, buxom, nubile, vivacious, pretty, curvaceous, fun-loving. But each time it was the same story.

"BLUE" PICTURES

With his sun-tanned torso and well-trimmed beard

(cont. p. 94)

MACMILLAN REMEMBERS

VOL 79

THE YEARS OF ANGUISH

(as seen on TV)

DAVID WOOD WRITES: Make no mistake about it, we shall never see his like again.

Compared with the puny dwarves of today he bestrides the post-war years like a colossus. Macmillan! The very word breathes of another, almost forgotten world - a world of style and elegance, when the sun shone, the band played under the elms, and Lily Langtry was the champagne toast of every masher in town. Try as he may, Mr Edward Heath cannot hope to recapture the swagger, the élan and the sheer imperial splendour of those far-off days. © Moggtrash Publications Inc. 1973

McKENZIE: Prime Minister, I believe you were in office for several years. I wonder if you can remember anything about those days ?

OLD JOLYON: Indeed I can. They were wonderful times, the happiest I can remember.

McKENZIE: Yet you must have been very worried by the ever-present threat of nuclear warfare ?

MACMILLAN: Oh yes. But I was very lucky. Our scientists had been able to devise an entirely new type of bomb, called the Skylon. The way it worked was very simple. You tied it up to a post. Then you lit the blue touch paper and retired.

McKENZIE: Well, I'd like to leave the events leading up to your retirement until next week, Mr Macmillan - but in the meantime, there was the Cuba crisis, wasn't there ?

MACMILLAN: Yes indeed. HOLDS UP COPY OF HIS MEMOIRS IN FRONT OF HIS FACE FOR FIVE MINUTES.

VOICE OVER: Yes, Harold Macmillan's sensational revelations are on sale now! Hurry, Hurry, while stocks last. Only two million copies printed. Order your copy now from Macmillans the publishers (no relation).

MACMILLAN: I shall never forget that week. We all thought it was the beginning of World War 3. It might well have been, if I had not been there to advise the young President, Jack Kennedy, on what to do.

McKENZIE (obviously surprised): You mean, you were actually advising the President at that time ?

MACMILLAN: Oh yes. I don't think it's ever been revealed before - (HOLDS UP BOOK AGAIN) but we were on the telephone all the time during that week. Of course it was quite awkward on occasions. You see, the Americans have different times to us. When we're just getting up for breakfast, for some reason or another they're having their luncheon. They like to do things differently from us. Of course this has never stood in the way of our two great countries getting together on a whole range of issues ....

McKENZIE: Z-z-z-z-z-z-z-z

MACMILLAN: Yes indeed. It's never been told before - but Jack Kennedy never put a foot wrong. He played his cards extremely well, and did everything I told him.

McKENZIE: But of course it wasn't all roses, was it Prime Minister? You were running into a lot of criticism at that time.

MACMILLAN: Oh yes. This is inevitable. They had this variety show - what was it called - *Beyond A Joke*. I went to see it once - very amusing.

McKENZIE: And there was the day when you sacked the whole Cabinet.

MACMILLAN: Oh yes, it was the most distressing episode of my life. (REACHES FOR HANDKERCHIEF).
I shall never forget that day. Just standing there and seeing a whole generation of ministers wiped out in a matter of minutes. Those of us who came through were never the same again. Poor Selwyn. He was a great loss. Incidentally, now that I have got my handkerchief out, would you mind asking me about the assassination of President Kennedy? (FISHES IN POCKET FOR ONION).

McKENZIE: Prime Minister, I'd like to turn now, if I may, to the sad events of November 1963.

MACMILLAN: Ah yes. It was the most distressing episode of my life. (BEGINS TO PEEL ONION WITH SMALL SILVER PENKNIFE).
I'd last seen young Jack Kennedy in the summer of that year. He flew over to stay with me - we used to sit here in this very room. It was a happy time. There were just the 300 or so of us staying here. Dean Rusk and Alec Home had to be be put out in the village, I remember. The sun shone, the band played under the old elm trees, there was the distant sound of bat on ball. And then one day came the terrible news. Some Archduke or other had been assassinated in Sarajevo. It didn't mean much to us at the time - but later, we all realised, that it was the end of the world we had known, and that things could never be the same again. (LAND OF HOPE AND GLORY SWELLS TO CLIMAX. CAMERA TRACKS AWAY TO SHOW AN OLD MAN SITTING IN HIS CHAIR, LOOKING INTO MIDDLE DISTANCE, TEARS STREAMING DOWN HIS FACE).

VOICE OVER: Next Week - The Profumo Affair - Macmillan Forgets.

Introduced by David Attenbore

The Wonderful World of Nature

Pt 17

Birds of New Neasden

Attenbore is discovered seated in absurd plastic chair in front of large TV screen.

ATTENBORE: Hullo again! This week The Wonderful World of Nature takes a look at the fascinating bird-life of the New Neasden archipelago. Before these islands were discovered a hundred years ago, more than a million different species of birds are thought to have lived there. They ranged from the mighty Tolkein's Auk, which stood over 12 feet high, to the smallest bird in the world, the tiny Olgakorbut.

[FILM OF MAN IN BEARD CUTTING HIS WAY THROUGH BUSH, WITH SOUND TRACK OF ENGLISH BIRD-SONG.]

ATTENBORE: Today there are only seven birds left on the little island of New Dollis Hill, and a team of scientists from the North Circular Polytechnic have been trying to find out why.

[FILM OF MAN IN BEARD OPERATING ENORMOUSLY COMPLICATED ELECTRONIC EQUIPMENT.]

ATTENBORE: Dr. Alan Sponge has spent the past 18 years trapping this little chap —the Yellow Blackbird. Once upon a time he was the commonest bird on the island. Dr. Sponge catches the birds with the aid of this highly-sophisticated electronic net.

[FILM OF BIRD FLYING INTO NET, AND MAN WITH BEARD RUNNING EXCITEDLY TOWARDS IT.]

ATTENBORE: When he has caught them, Dr. Sponge first of all places these multi-coloured metal discs round their legs, each of them numbered.

[FILM OF MAN WITH BEARD CLUTCHING BIRD AND PLACING LARGE METAL DISCS ON EACH LEG.]

ATTENBORE: He then places minute electrodes in their brains to record their song. And this is where the US Navy comes in.

[FILM OF AIRCRAFT CARRIER. CUT TO HUNDREDS OF AMERICAN SAILORS SITTING IN FRONT OF BANKS OF ELECTRONIC EQUIPMENT.]

ATTENBORE: When he has cut off their wings, Dr. Sponge releases the blackbirds and they hop off back into the bush. So far few have survived for more than a few days, but Dr. Sponge is sure that one day he will solve the mystery of why these rare and beautiful little birds are nearly extinct.

Next week we shall take a look at Heinz Bakedbeenz's astonishing film of the Giant Hamsters of Lithuania. Good night.

"Then the girl kissed the frog and it turned into Trotsky."

FILM OF PREVIN LIFE PLANNED

by Our Film Reporter
'BINKIE' GAUMONT

The famous Italian film director Franco "Zeff" O'Relli, a distant relative of the world famous Neasden footballer is to make a film based on the life of the 20th century conductor Andre Previn.

O'Relli, 49, will begin filming later this year in the Sutton and Cheam district of Greater London

Beautiful

Provisionally entitled *St Francis of A Go Go* the film tells the story of the very wonderful Andre who gave up everything to devote his life to music.

O'Relli (no relation) has chosen a young Newport Pagnell sixth-former to play the lead part of Andre.

He is sixteen year old Raymond Prattwinkle, the son of a former whisky salesman.

Very Wonderful

Raymond's co-star, who plays Andre's travelling companion Mia, will be pretty shorthand typist Lana Limmits also from Newport Pagnell.

It has been "Zeff" O'Relli's life time ambition to tell in movie terms the very wonderful and moving story of Andre, the simple Californian boy who forsook a life of poverty to become a world famous conductor.

"To me" says O'Relli, "Andre is a symbol of innocence. Somehow his life has become an example for people of all ages who follow him on the concert platform and on TV."

Zeff O'Relli is 57.

A DAY IN THE LIFE OF RADIO NEASDEN

Reg Wibble:.... Well, by my watch, it's 3.49 in the morning, and I imagine most of you by now are asleep. But in case you're not, this is Reg Wibble and Radio Neasden bringing you eight hours of non-stop news, views and time checks. Well, the clock on the wall says it's 3.50, and that means there's only another two hours and ten minutes before it's six o' clock, when it'll be time for the Monty Wiven's Show, But meanwhile this is Reg Wibble with another two hours of......

Telephone: Brrr-Brrr. Brrr-Brrr.

Wibble:....Wait a minute. That sounds like the telephone. That means we've got someone on the line. Remember, you too can phone in, twenty four hours a day..

Telephone: Brrr-Brrr.

Wibble:....Make a note of the number - you can ring into Radio Neasden at 01 - that's 01 (but of course you don't need that if you're already in the London dialling area...

Telephone: Brrr- Brrr.

Wibble:....so the number to ring is just 353...damn, I've lost it...hang on a minute .. Oh, of course it's on this telephone that's ringing here...

Telephone Rings Off.

Wibble:....Oh bleep! It's stopped ringing.

Telephone: Brrr-Brrr.

Wibble:...Hallo.

Caller:...Hullo, is that you Mr. Wibble?

Wibble: ...Yes, it's Reg Wibble here...but can you hold on for a minute, caller, I'm afraid we've got to take a break here. We'll be back with you in just a moment.

Music: Plink, plonk, plunk.

Breathy Voice: ... Aren't you asleep yet? You must be desperate, if you're still listening to this rubbish. Try counting sheep. So soft, so woolly. You know they make sense! 1 - 2 - 3 - Zzzzz. Sheep! The answer to a good night's sleep!

PLINK PLUNK PLONK

Wibble:....You're tuned in to Neasden Radio, and this is Reg Wibble, with news of the latest weather. Well, I'm just looking out of the window, and to tell you the truth, it's so dark that I can't even make out whether it's still raining or not. Hang on, I'll just go over to the window and put my hand out.

Telephone: Brrr-Brrr.

Caller:....Hullo, is that Radio Neasden? This is Mrs Doris Grobe speaking.

Wibble....Hullo, Mrs Grobe, and thank you for calling. A very good morning to you - and what can we do for you?

Mrs Grobe:....Well, I live upstairs, at 36, and my husband and I are sick to death of you opening and shutting the window every five minutes. Why don't you go to sleep, like everyone else ?

Wibble:....Thank you, caller, and now we take a break, and go over to the Radio Neasden newsdesk for a look at the latest world headlines at this moment in time.... that's 6.35 a.m. Just hold on a minute while I carry the microphone across....

Music: Bing, bong, bing, bong.

Wibble:....This is Radio Neasden, and here is Reg Wibble with the very latest news. We've just heard on the BBC that President Nixon resigned yesterday. So for a latest up-to-the-minute report on the situation, over to our Special Washington Correspondent Reg Wibble.

PLINK PLONK

Wibble:....Well, this is certainly sensational news. If the BBC reports are to be believed, it clearly looks as though the President of the United States has resigned. The situation is certainly confused, and what people here are waiting to see now is the morning paper.

PLINK PLONK

Telephone: Brrr-Brrr.

Operator:....Is dat 353-8111? Dis am your early mornin' alarm call, suh!

Wibble:....Oh, thank you. That means it's time for me to go to bed now, so I'll hand you over to your host for the next four hours, Monty Wivens.

Wivens:....Thank you, Reg. This is Radio Neasden, and this is your host for the next four hours, Monty Wivens, Well, the time now by our studio clock is 7.24, and the latest weather news is that it is still raining. So let's kick off with a look at the morning's papers. But just before we do that, it's time for a break.

Music: Bing - Bong - Bung.

Voice:....For weddings and bar-mitzvahs! - JARVIS, Neasden's Number One Photographer at 847 2191. If he's not in, his Granny will take a message. JARVIS - You know it makes sense.

Music: BLINK - BLONK - BLUNK

Wivens:....And now the time is 8.33, it's still raining, and time for Hullo Listeners, Radio Neasden's morning round-up of news and views, with of course regular time and weather checks, not to mention latest traffic news from Neasden's busy North Circular, in which I'm joined by my colleague Janet Office-Cleaner. Hi there Jan!

Office -Cleaner:....Blimeyoreilly, corstrikealight, stonetheblee-epingcrows, what ableepblee-pmess you've got in 'ere and no mistake! 'Ow the 'eck d' you fink I'm 'xpected to keep this lot nice and tidylike, with all these flippin' wires and tapes and fag ends all

over the flippin' plice?

Wivens:....And now Janet Office-Cleaner brings you the latest weather and news.

Music: Kerploink, kerplunk.

Office-Cleaner:....Gorblimey, it's fair comin' down cats and dogs out there. Looks as if it's set in for the day, if you ask me. I told my old man this morning, Reg, I said, you better take your mac with you this morning, I said. And talking of going to work, you should 'ave seen the traffic when I came in this morning. It was so thick down Tesco Road I had to wait all of half an hour for a 97.

Wivens: ....That was Janet Office-Cleaner with latest traffic and weather news......

Office-Cleaner....'ang on a sec, love, I 'aven't finished yet. As I was saying, I was standin' there waitin' for a flipping 97, when I saw this bloke fall off his bike. It fair gave me a nasty turn, I can tell you.

Wivens:....That was a late local news flash. But now let's turn to ...er...um... oh, yes, entertainment news. I see here in *Time Out* that there's a Gay Lib demonstration on Saturday... oh, hang on, that's last week's. Janet, have you seen the latest *Time Out?*

Office-Cleaner:....Garn, I threw all them rubbishy old newspapers out of the window a few minutes ago...a lot of rubbish about that poor David Nixon and the White House scandal.

Wivens:....Well so much for today's international news headlines. And now here is a police message.

Inspector Knacker *(for it is he)*: We have just heard that a man has been struck on the head by a large pile of newspapers and magazines. The accident took place in the vicinity of the offices of Radio Neasden. Would

anyone who can help the police with their enquiries please ring this number.. 353 8111.

Wivens:....And now, for the next few hours, we have readings from some of the best classified advertisements in yesterday's *Evening News.* Here's one for a start.

Janet:..."Office Cleaner required, new Broadcasting Company in N. London. Good speaking voice essential...."

(Contd. 94 khtzvhf)

Poetry Corner

Forthcoming Marriage

Jeremy Thorpe and Marion, Countess of Harewood.

Congratulations to you both
On this memorable
Occasion.

So. It was
The love of music
That drew you together.
It is really terrific
When two people
Are brought together
By a common interest.

You, Jeremy, play the violin
A fact which has
Only come to light
Recently as far as
I'm concerned.

You, Marion, are a former
Concert pianist.

Greetings then
Liberal leader and former
Royal consort.

Keith's mum
Apparently
Thinks
That it's all a
Bit too soon after
His tragic bereavement.

But things have changed a lot
Since Keith's mum was young.

ERIC JARVIS THRIBB (17)

*"Go on - beat the lights - Syd would have
wanted it that way"*

*"How dare you talk like that to the woman
I'm shacking up with."*

" 'School of Harold Lloyd' ?"

Lord Gnome owns 10 Michaelangelos~ shouldn't you

GRAFFITI   *Mervyn Rubbisch*

Using the technique of web-offset photolithography for the very first time, the very wonderful and highly important young artist Mervyn Rubbisch has created this original work of art SPECIALLY FOR YOU!

Since his arrival in this country in 1935, Rubbisch has become a household word. His paintings command astronomical prices. His 2000' long mural *'A History of Neasden'* was universally acclaimed when it was unveiled in the Milton Keynes Community Centre last year by the Duchess of Kent, as part of the 'Twenty Five Years of Stevenage New Town' Festival.

Now, thanks to Lord Gnome, you have a unique opportunity to possess an original work of art by Rubbisch in the privacy of your own home.

We would like to emphasise that this is not just an ordinary reproduction, but an Original and Very Important Work of Art, in its own right.

Only 2,000,000 copies of Rubbisch's *'Graffiti'* have been 'pulled', from Rubbisch's own lovingly-prepared 'master plate'. The moment that this stock has been sold, the 'master plate' will be destroyed, thereby ensuring that your print of *'Graffiti'* remains UNIQUE FOREVER!

Among the other ORIGINAL WORKS which will be enriching your home in the months to come are:

Sid Cockney's 'HULLO SAILOR'. Cockney is that rare cross between the primitive and the mentally disturbed which makes so much of modern art what it is today. He studied at Portsmouth between 1947 and 1955 under A.B. "Butch" Rothenstein R.N. His work has been seen in Cardiff, the Arndale Centre Sheffield, and Gay Magazine.

Elizabeth Crank's 'PORTRAIT OF R. HALL ESQ.' Crank is one of the most exciting talents of her generation, and millions of visitors to Coventry Cathedral will have gasped at her 'Mandala '62', an evocation in pre-stressed Fibron of the horror of Auschwitz. She lives in the Camargue in an upturned fishing boat, and wears old sailors' vests.

have at least one ?

of these very wonderful and original works of art

We would like to stress that these very wonderful and Important Works of Art are not just a load of over-priced rubbish, but a Very Important Investment Opportunity, of the type you should not miss.

In selecting the graphics illustrated above, we have acted on the advice of a team of experts including Sir Cyril Kleinwort, Mr. Samuel Montague and Sir Max Rayne.

Barbara Woolworth's 'THREE PIECE SUIT'. Miss Woolworth is internationally famous as an heiress who has been married at least seven times. She is less well known for her lithography, inspired by the gnarled relics of plastic detergent bottles which she finds on the beaches of her native Cornwall. The 'Three Piece Suit', a set of four individual prints - 'Old Bottle', 'Another Old Bottle' and 'Bugger Me, That Makes Three of Them' - constitutes a meaningful statement about the effects of environmental pollution on a Cornish beach.

Monty Pirelli's 'ROXANE 32-21-36'. Pirelli's highly-charged eroticism has a formal elegance which has excited the attention of, among others, Lord Clark and Inspector 'Knacker of the Yard'Knacker. Pirelli uses the images of pornography to make a profound statement about the ambivalent nature of reality today.

* *

☐ Please send me 1/10/25 copies of Rubbisch's Very Unique and Important *'Graffiti'*. (£325 each exc. VAT).

☐ Crank's *'Badger Reclining'* (£231, exc. VAT).

☐ Cockney's *'Hullo Sailor'* (£750, exc. VAT).

☐ Woolworth's *'Detergent Bottles'* (£250, exc VAT).

If you do not require frames, chosen by the Design Centre and made by Fabrika Poulsen Ltd. of Copenhagen (£84 each), please say so.

NAME..............................
ADDRESS.........................

Christie's (Gnome) Ltd., Christie, Manson and Woods, 8 King Street, S.W.1.

* *

Sir John ~ New poem shock

by Glenda Strobes

The Poet Laureate Sir John Thribb has written a new poem, he told me over lunch at the Savoy today.

It is entitled *'The Last Antirrhinum of Summer'* and it describes Sir John's feelings on catching a glimpse of Mr Duncan Sandys on his way to a board meeting of the controversial Lonrho international conglomerate.

"I don't suppose it's much good?" Sir John confided over the Lobster Boudin de Honfleur, "but put it in, won't you? I could do with the money."

Here then is Sir John's first full-length verse drama since becoming Poet Laureate.

LENTEN THOUGHTS OF A HIGH ANGLICAN AFTER A FEW SCHOONERS OF NEASDILLADO BRITISH-TYPE CYPRUS SHERRY

Lovely lady in the pew,
Goodness, what a scorcher - phew!
What I wouldn't give to do
Unmentionable things to you.

If old God is still up there
I'm sure he wouldn't really care.
I'm sure he'd say "A little lech
Never really harmed old Betj."

Sir John is 91.

Anne sees Giant Vole

by LUNCHTIME O'BOOZE
Ethiopia Tues.

Princess Anne today came face to face with the very rare Ethiopean Giant Yellow Vole, the only one of its kind in the world.

The incident occurred during Day 2 of the Princess' Royal Safari in the famed McWeidenfeld Mountains named after the 18th century Scottish explorer.

AMAZING

"Gosh, isn't it big?" said Anne with a flash of her father's wit. "Is it a he or a she."

No one seemed to know. But native

Game Warden Wally Mpoulson told the Princess "If you know a better vole, go to it."

Princess Anne later watched fascinated as the luckless Mpoulson was fed to the famed Ethiopian lions.

SURPRISE

After a breakfast consisting of grapefruit segments, cornflakes, haddocks, egg, bacon, sausage, fried bread, tomato and mushroom, the Princess mounted a bingo -- a cross between an ostrich and a giraffe -- and set off on a sogat hunting expedition.

The sogat is a small beaver-like animal with razor sharp fur.

Later the Princess watched a native display of television in the Maudling Lounge of the Ethiopian Hilton.

The Queen is 40.

with
BAMBER GASKET

There are few things in life that can compare with the pleasurable glow of anticipation with which the holidaying motorist approaches the Motorway.

As through the dreary back streets or B roads he wends his weary way, his eyes ever and anon light upon those tiny blue Roadside 'M' signs that betoken the close proximity of that magical thing which has for for a good ten years or so captured the imagination of man's adventurous spirit. England has always been a Motorway-going nation and I like to think that there is not one of us who does not have the blood of the motorway running through his veins.

As the motorist comes ever nearer through T junction and one-way system, he can sniff in his nostrils the unmistakable tang and hear the immemorial rumble of articulated lorries in the distance. Then, suddenly, he rounds a bend and there she is in all her majesty! That endless expanse of grey-blue tarmac stretching away to the horizon calling.....calling....whither? Who knows?

As Old Jowett has it:

"I must go down to the Motorway
To the four-lane stretch and the spaghetti
junction
And all I ask is a souped-up Jag
And an overdrive that will function in all
conditions."

(Carshalton Casualty Tent
A 463 Tues.)

Tiny Genius rocks Universe Shock

by Our Science Correspondent
PATRICK BORE

Make no mistake about it. Since last week's sensational Dimbleby Bore-In appearance by 22-year-old Israeli-born Uri Nargs the universe as we know it will never be the same again.

Not since Sir Isaac Newton shot the apple off his son's head at the age of two and a half, has the world of science been so rocked to its foundations.

From the moment Uri succeeded in bending a common-or-garden teaspoon in front of 15 million TV viewers, hard-bitten scientists have had to throw out almost every existing theory about the way the world works — not to mention their cutlery.

MINDBENDER

For thousands of years, scientists have argued that spoons are straight.

Now they are queuing up in droves to examine the ordinary Israeli bus-driver who has proved them wrong.

SENSATION

Says Dr.E.Pockmaker, head of the prestigious Gnome Institute for Advanced Time-Wasting On Large Grants. "What we have seen here is perhaps the biggest break-through in pure science since Hugh Cudlipp invented the 72 pt. four-letter word." *(See Cudlipp, Man of Destiny, p.94 —ED)*

"Of course we scientists could not possibly consider 15 million viewers as a sufficiently representative sample to prove this thing one way or the other."

But as Dr.Pockmaker, 42, explains: "There are some things we scientists just cannot explain — such as why we get huge grants to research into ridiculous things like this.

"Ideally I would like to spend 50 years working with Mr. Nargs under proper scientific conditions."

Another scientist, Professor Branestawm, of the Heath Robinson Parapsychology Unit at the University of Neasden, believes that Uri's powers could be harnessed to solve the world's growing energy crisis.

Says Branestawm, 85: "There is no reason, speaking scientifically, why Mr. Nargs could not generate enough electricity to light a small town.

"But ideally I would like to work with him for 74 years under proper scientific conditions before we could come to any definite conclusion on this."

Your Guide to the twilight world of Para~ psychology

by Dr.Brian No-Spikka-de-Inglis

Now that the universe will never be the same again, here are some of the terms which will be coming into everyday currency soon.

TELEPATHY: disease of the mind caused by watching TV programmes on para-psychology.
PARA-NORMAL: heterosexual member of

Uri Nargs

airborne division.

GHOST: figure with white sheet over head going 'oooooo'.

ALAN BRIEN: man possessed with hypnotic gift — i.e. able to send millions to sleep simply by writing words on paper.

OUIJA: Common Market word meaning 'yes' in French and German simultaneously.

ESP: abbreviation for Extra Silly Person — i.e. one who writes this sort of rubbish, e.g. Alan Brien Inglis etc.

ON OTHER PAGES:
Your Spoons Tonight . . . p. 49

LETTERS TO THE EDITOR

Those spoons

From Sir Herbert Gussett

Sir,   Sir Arthur Koestler, in his fascinating article "Believe It Or Not", appealed for readers to send in their personal experiences of inexplicable phenomena. What follows is an accurate account of something which actually happened at my home, The Old Maltings, Malby Crofton, Herts, at precisely 11.03 pm. on the evening of last Friday, 23 November.

I was seated in front of the television set, in the company of my lady wife, watching a programme about some foreign pop-singer chappie doing some damfool tricks with spoons. Well, I've been out East a few times, and I can tell you I wasn't fooled for a minute. I remember one night out in India, one of my fellow-officers did some amazing things with a pack of playing cards, a banana and a goat which I would hesitate to describe in mixed company.

But anyway, there I was watching this fellow on the old goggle-box, when suddenly, for no clear reason, there came into my mind a very distinct picture of a large tumbler, filled with whisky. Strange to relate, the tumbler was exactly like one of the ones we keep in our sideboard.

I found myself mysteriously impelled, as if by some strange power beyond my ken, to rise from my chair and walk towards the sideboard.

At the exact moment when I was reaching out my hand for the bottle, I heard a most almighty crash from the hall outside. "That's deuced odd," I thought to myself, since there was no one else in the house apart from my lady wife and myself, and anyway she was asleep in front of the TV, and had been since "Crown Court" the afternoon before.

Now comes the really extraordinary part, which I offer to Professor Koestler for what it's worth. I opened the door to discover the prostrate form of my old friend Lt. Col. 'Buffy' Frobisher. He was lying in the hall, having tripped over my old mahogany hat and umbrella stand, which had come crashing down on him as he fell. It seems, from what Buffy could remember of the incident the next day, that he had been sitting in the Berni Bar of the Coach and Forte, just before closing time, when he remembered that he had come out in the first place to borrow a cup of sugar for his wife's tea. Now I ask Professor Koestler to pay particular attention to what follows. Buffy had set off and walked towards my home, a journey which he knows well. He could have arrived at any moment during the evening. I am no mathematician, but I would think that the odds against him arriving at precisely that moment must have been 10,000 million to one.

Yours faithfully,
H. GUSSETT
Gussett Institute for the Investigation of Para-Alcoholic Phenomena,
Much Boozing,
Wilts.

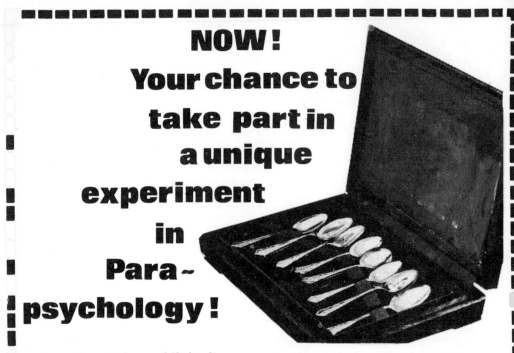

KNEE: IS IT THE END FOR RON'S NEASDEN ?

asks DUD FIVERS
Soccer's MR FOOTBALL

The shock 17-0 defeat of Neasden United by plucky non-leaguers Dagenham Geriatrics last Saturday once again spelt out the age old question:

ARE NEASDEN FINISHED?

That was the question I put to an ashen-faced Ron Knee, Neasden's tight-lipped supremo, seconds after he and his men had walked down the tunnel of despair following the defeat they are calling the Dagenham Disaster.

Penalty

Make no mistake. Behind his tight lips and ashen-face Knee is a worried man.

For he knows in his heart of hearts that this star-studded side which has been compared with such all-time greats as Sanitas of Brazil and the Moscow Sparkplugs, is now over the hill.

Tragedy

Is it the end of the road for men like legendary No 4 shirt Ken Essoldo, 51, the former Gibraltarian International whose name was once synonymous with Great Football?

"Ken couldn't find his form I agree" admitted Knee, 59, "For that matter he couldn't find his support, and I don't mean Sid and Doris."

Disgust

Saturday's showdown has left a searing question mark hanging over the head of 62-year-old Neasden net-minder Wally Foot.

Time and time again the Dagenham strikers made the one-legged Foot look like an old man curled up asleep 'in the corner of the goal.

"I had been up all night with some mates playing cards" frankly admitted the man they used to call 'the Baboon' from the way he could swing between the goal-posts with astonishing agility.

Pathos

Before the match Knee boasted that his Brains-in-Boots Bert O'Relli would run rings round the Dagenham defence.

But for all we saw of him he could have been playing somewhere else.

"He was playing somewhere else" growled Knee "this lad has a looming question mark hanging over his Neasden shirt."

Ron Knee is 59.

"Basically I like it but take out the carrot"

RICH!

THE INCREDIBLE STORY OF HOW A YOUNG ROMAN CATHOLIC NOVELIST, PURE PORN READ, **BECAME SO DESPERATE FOR MONEY THAT HE BROKE ALL MORAL CODES AND WROTE ABOUT THE ONE SUBJECT THAT STILL REMAINED TABOO—CANNIBALISM.**

Part Four

THE TRUTH DAWNS

by Andes Previn

The room was bitterly cold. From the kitchen he could hear his wife walking with heavy feet. The lack of money was at last beginning to tell. The royalties from his books **The Randy Monk** and **The Pervert** had finally run out.

The cold winter wind had brought heavy snow to Hampstead. Pure Porn knew that it was just a matter of time before the inevitable end.

That evening they discussed, again, the courses open to them. Despite their condition, they felt strangely elated. Beryl sometimes laughed, but it was a hollow laugh. After a little time she began to cry again. "I can't go on", she told him repeatedly. "I can't I can't."

All along in the back of his mind Pure Porn had known that there was a way out for them, but so far he had not dared to mention it to Beryl. It was hard enough, even for him, to accept it. Now for the first time he told her about it.

"I am going to write a book about cannibalism" he said. His voice was strangely calm. "I will go into all the details. People will say how can you, a Catholic, do such a thing? But Our Lord was never opposed to people making a killing, when there was no other way."

Beryl began to cry again. "Can you be so sure that this horrible deed will save us?" Her voice showed stress.

Patiently he explained to her how he knew that what he was going to do would save them. He was, after all, a very successful writer. He knew which were the spicy bits and which bits were of no use.

As calmly as he could he told Beryl that he would do it all quite quickly and that it would sustain them indefinitely, possibly for many years.

The following day they took the first rolls of notes from Secker and Warburg. They were still fresh. They looked crisp and green. He gave some to Beryl and she reluctantly accepted them.

Read stuffed as many as he could into his wallet. Slowly he felt the strength returning to him.

NEXT WEEK:
A Huge Advance—Film Rights—Observer Serialisation.

THE GNOME GUIDE TO A MILLION YEARS OF CHINESE ART

FOR OVER A MILLION YEARS, EXPERTS HAVE BEEN FASCINATED BY THE UNKNOWN WORLD THAT IS CHINA. CENTURIES BEFORE THE BIRTH OF MARCO POLO, THESE UNIQUE PEOPLES WERE READING NEWSPAPERS, FLYING THROUGH THE AIR WITH THE HELP OF WATER-POWERED KITES AND EATING FROZEN TAKEAWAY CHOP SUEY. TODAY FOR THE VERY FIRST TIME WE ARE IN A UNIQUE POSITION TO ASSESS AND EVALUATE THE UNIQUE CONTRIBUTION THAT THE CIVILISATION WE CALL CHINA HAS MADE TO THE CULTURAL HERITAGE OF MANKIND.

HISTORY OF CHINA

It was the Emperor What-Son (2191-2184) who once cut down a mulberry tree and was eaten alive by the Holy Dragon of Wo-king. Thus began the terrible "War of the Seven Kingdoms" which lasted over 2000 years, and cost the lives of over 600 million people.

It was however the celebrated Emperor Wil-Son who finally dragged modern China as we know it today kicking and screaming into the 7th. century BC.

Wil-Son was in every sense an enlightened ruler. He overthrew the wicked landlords, distributed the great wealth of the merchants to the poor peasants, and in the words of his Chief Eunuch Hee-Lee, "made the honourable rich men squeal like pigs."

Wil-Son's wife, the Empress Glad-ys, was one of China's most celebrated poets. One of her more poignant verses has survived to this day, and tells us something of life at the imperial court in that distant age: *The ducks fly up the wall*
Nimmo the imperial cat
Slumbers by the fire.
It is Win-car-nis time.
The time when all men are happy
And the troubles of the day are forgotten.

In 141, China was again wracked by the so-called War of the Water Buffalo. It is perhaps the supreme irony that this period was one of extraordinary artistic achievement, seeing as it did the famous Bronze Grasshoppers of Won-Nee (59 BC), and the now world-famous Jade Plastic Beaker Disposal Unit of Heeth-Ko.

PING DYNASTY. Teapot. Probably the oldest known teapot in the world. Given as a birthday present to the Princess An-An by its maker Tet-Lee, who was later beheaded for putting the imperial milk in first. (4191 BC). Green faience with double-fired glaze. Notice the spout. It really pours!

PONG DYNASTY. Ambergris vase in the shape of a hippopotamus. Found in cave near Neas-Den during Cultural Revolution. This priceless object is the only one of its type in the world.

MOGG DYNASTY. Long-playing record, the work of El-Pee (33½ BC), who gave his name to this astonishing feat of scientific invention, which was unfortunately useless owing to the failure of contemporary attempts to invent the gramophone. The record is made out of crushed bean shoots held together by finely woven gold threads.

BUNG-HO DYNASTY. The priceless Ron-Son golden Burial Ashtray from the Grave of the 809 Kings. The Chinese believed that the first thing a dead king wanted when he arrived in the 'Garden of the Seventeenth Celestial Happiness' was 'a smoke'. Royal tombs often contained thousands of cigarette papers, and enough tobacco to last a lifetime.

THE TAI-PING PAPER. The Chinese invented paper, and this fragment, recently discovered on a rubbish tip outside Peking, is believed to be the earliest known example in the history of the world. Experts have managed to decipher the cryptic message · "Your dynasty's in the oven."

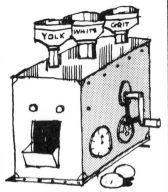

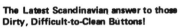

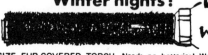